# YEARNING FOR GOD

REFLECTIONS OF FAITHFUL LIVES

Margaret Ann Crain
&
Jack Seymour

with
**Group Discussion Guide**

UPPER
ROOM BOOKS®
NASHVILLE

Cover and Interior Design: Christa Schoenbrodt/Studio Haus
Cover Photo: Andrea Sperling/Getty Images
First Printing: 2003

**Library of Congress Cataloging-in-Publication Data**
Crain, Margaret Ann.
Yearning for God : reflections of faithful lives / Margaret Ann Crain and Jack L.
    Seymour.
    p.    cm.
ISBN 0-8358-0991-9
1. Christian biography—United States. I. Seymour, Jack L. (Jack Lee), 1948–
II. Title.
BR1700.3 .C73 2003
277.3'082'0922—dc21                                        2002013294

Printed in the United States of America

To all those who so generously shared their faith with us.
We stood together on holy ground.

# CONTENTS

# PREFACE

We often begin lectures or workshops with the invitation "Take off your shoes, for we're standing on holy ground." Our lectures are peppered with stories that laypeople have so generously shared with us, accounts of their yearnings for God. We listened as they struggled to name the theological questions and yearnings for God that the twists and turns of life have raised. We truly believe that through our interviews with laypersons—interviews that were the source of the insights in this book—we have encountered the grace of God. God is present in the stories of these faithful individuals.

Nearly forty men and women agreed to meet with us and tell us the story of their lives. Telling one's life story usually takes two or three hours. Often tears come when memories are painful. Yet, over and over, these people affirmed God's presence in their lives.

As they recounted their histories, they connected with the presence of the Holy One who loves, forgives, guides, and challenges us. They touched the questions, many unresolved, at the heart of the faith that guides them. They told how the church and its resources of theology, stories, and practices empowered them.

They also talked about areas where the church let them down by not providing the help they needed. They shared stories of the faithful people who supported, mentored, and sent them forward. It is indeed holy ground to be in God's presence and to witness how God has worked and offered new life to an individual.

We promised each storyteller anonymity, yet everyone we interviewed shared freely. Many persons gave us permission to use their real names and locations. They willingly participated, grateful for an opportunity to share their theological questions with caring listeners. "No one has ever listened to all this before," they often said as the interview ended. "Thank you for listening." We found these people hungering for an opportunity to reflect on the meaning of their lives and relationship with God through deep and thorough conversation.

We have tried to protect the privacy of persons we interviewed by using pseudonyms and changing geographic locations and other details. These people come from congregations located in the Southeast, Midwest, and eastern seaboard of the United States. They are all from mainstream Protestant churches.

We thank them for the gifts they have given us—gifts of friendship, truth telling, and insight. We thank them for being so gracious and willing in their desire to help others in the journey of faith, meaning, and vocation.

This group is not intended to represent anything except themselves. Because we took focused time to hear their faith stories in such depth, we believe that you may hear echoes of your own life history and theological questions as you read these stories. The value of such a book as this one is that in hearing these persons' stories, you may be prompted to tell stories of your own.

In our stories is embedded the story of God's presence. In our stories we discover the questions we need to ask in order to grow in our relationship with God. We discover guidance for our lives. We may discover the meanings that have guided us even when all seemed meaningless. We may identify new meaning for a different phase of living.

The yearnings we identified from the stories we were privileged to hear are undoubtedly not the only yearnings of persons in relation to faith experience. They are simply the yearnings that seemed uppermost to this group of people. We invite you to think of other yearnings that are important for you. Find a group of people with whom you can share your yearnings and their accompanying questions. We call this process of sharing life stories, yearnings, and finding meaning *theological reflection*.

Finally, we hope and pray that this book and its promptings will help you to re-form your congregation so that storytelling, listening for God's presence in each person's story, and reflecting on the meaning of each story will become a regular part of your life together. What better place can we find to ask the theological questions we yearn to address than in a gathering of the people of God, with all the wisdom of the Judeo-Christian tradition present?

# 1

## LIFE-SHAPED FAITH
### Theology in Everyday Life

As the door opened, in walked a spry and slim older man, professionally dressed. Though eighty-seven years old, Frederick looked about sixty-five. A smile of vitality and energy crossed his face. He was looking forward to this invitation to converse about his family and his faith.

At Frederick's core is a thirst for learning. He has taught Sunday school for over sixty years and continues to lead a class every Sunday. Even a couple of years before retiring from the personnel department of a major public utility, he attended "sensitivity group" training for managers. He said of the training, "We did something there that gave me keys to doors and opened other doors and extended this business of curiosity. . . . It opened up for me, for the first time, an intellectual examination of feelings. I knew I had feelings, but I never thought about them."

Yes, "this business of curiosity," as Frederick calls it, draws him into new experiences. He remembers taking several training courses in "public affairs" and "human relations" during his final years of employment. These classes opened up areas of reflection and commitment. Even with all of this searching, he wants others to know that "it's really hard to pull things together." Yet that is exactly what he is trying to do.

Full of vigor and searching, Frederick says, "I have a lot of outside interests in addition to the Active Seniors group [a church program for older adults], caregivers' meetings at the hospital, Alzheimer's groups from time to time, the Sunday school class. I work out at the Y three mornings a week, and I volunteer at the Red Cross and the telephone blood bank. I've got a lot of things to keep me active and interested. Then there is our large and busy family."

Frederick knew we were inquiring about the importance of faith and religion in his life. Before our conversation, he jotted down topics and experiences he did not want to forget and brought pictures to remind him of key influences in his life. He looked forward to the interview as another chance to extend "this business of curiosity" and to make sense of the events of his life.

Deeply trusting of life, Frederick does not fear exploring anything—his failures, losses, hopes, ethics, and confusion. "I think we religious folks would say that the most important thing is to help a person acquire a relationship with God, but that is really advanced by enthusiasm for learning." For him, the search for God coincides with openness to learning and searching. While he has endured loss and hurt, Frederick remains open to life and grounded in faith and trust. "As long as I can remember, I have felt a power in my life, which I now feel is the Holy Spirit." A bit embarrassed by that admission, he adds, "But I feel it is natural, not unnatural. How can I convey its naturalness to people without them feeling like—well, this fellow, he's a little overboard on religion? It bothers me that I don't know how to do that."

## REFLECTION

*What person or persons do you know who seem to speak easily about matters of faith or religion? How do you feel when you are with people like this? With whom do you find yourself able to share your faith?*

The losses are real. When Frederick was only five, his father died in a buggy accident. Upon the heels of this loss, the family lost their home. They moved in with a widowed grandmother whose household was filled with love but also rigid rules. Then Frederick's brother died in his teens from diabetes, just one year before the discovery of insulin. Accidents seem to plague the family; three sons-in-law also died from accidents.

When we talked, Frederick faced one of the most difficult times of his life. An accident had sped the progress of Alzheimer's in his beloved wife, Joy, to whom he had been married for over sixty years. Joy had possessed a "zest for life." She taught him "joyful living," yet now she lay in an Alzheimer's-induced coma in a hospital bed in their living room. Frederick and a daughter took turns caring for her. They expended heroic efforts to keep her comfortable and at home.

Because of Joy was experiencing seizures and could not eat, her family had decided, on the advice of an optimistic doctor, to have a feeding tube inserted. The doctor had assured them that Joy probably would return to her recent state of health in which she was "mobile, partially articulate, partially knew what was going on. She could eat or be fed and sit in family gatherings and 'enjoy' herself." But that had not happened. After the feeding tube was inserted, she never came out of the coma. She has quieted and they have brought her home. Yet, each day she lies in the living room of their home, seemingly unaware of what is going on around her, receiving nourishment through a tube. Frederick describes the situation:

> This matter of Joy's illness—now, this is causing problems in the family. Everyone agrees that Joy would not want to continue this way. The suggestion has been made to remove her feeding tube. I couldn't do that—take the overt step that would lead to her death.

Deep in his heart, where trust and tears come together, Frederick asks why. Why does Joy suffer? Why is family conflict

building about her care? Where is God? He muses: "I feel that if
God wants to take her, I will certainly acquiesce in that decision,
and there would be some measure of thankfulness. Some say I
should act as God's agent. I don't feel appointed to do that. But [the
situation] is causing friction."

Almost lamenting, Frederick turns to us and makes a profound
statement, articulating a question at the heart of faith.
"Somehow," he says, "*we have not made it possible or easy for people to
be theological in their everyday lives.*" He seeks to understand God's
love, grace, and hope in the midst of hurt and loss. He looks for
God's purposes.

Why don't we help one another know and follow God? That
question puzzles Frederick because he knows he needs help with
this task, and he wants to help others know and follow God. He reflects on a relationship with a friend from work:

> I had a friend who worked with me off and on in the
> company. He and I became pretty good friends, not social
> friends, but office friends. When he retired, I came to his
> retirement party. At that time, he declared that one of the
> strongest influences on his life had been his relationship
> with Jesus Christ. I told him afterwards, "I didn't know
> that." He said, "Well, it's my fault; I should have commu-
> nicated it." Then I realized that I had not told him about
> myself either. And I thought, *We were two fellows working
> closely together, and we never communicated our faith to each other.*
> I'm still puzzled that we didn't do that. There's some ele-
> ment of privacy—you don't want to sound sanctimo-
> nious, or you feel like the business area is not the place for
> religion. . . . People don't talk about [their faith] except on
> Sunday or in Sunday school. And yet it's the dominant el-
> ement in so many of our lives. Why aren't we able to com-
> municate it?

Communication about faith is the heart of vocation for him. "So one of my aims has been to try to bring this subject into communications, where we can talk not religion but theology, about our relationship with God." This idea confronts Frederick each time he sees Joy, holds her hand, and asks why.

## REFLECTION

*With what friends or colleagues do you speak easily about faith issues? Why is it easy to share faith questions with those persons?*

# Where Tears and Faith Come Together

Frederick articulates well the issues of meaning and purpose that stimulate and inform his faith. We all seek meaning, purpose, and hope in facing the joys, relationships, tasks, and hurts of life. Sometimes we encounter circumstances that stretch all of our resources; at other times, resources for finding meaning and responding seem readily available.

We asked the following questions of laypersons, ranging from sixteen to ninety years old, in seven congregations and in four states:

- How does life experience call people to theological and spiritual reflection?

- How does thinking about their faith empower people to live faithfully every day?

- What resources from faith and life do people use to make sense of their lives and to inspire their living?

- How do people engage in theological reflection in the ordinary moments of living?

• How do we draw meaning from the stories and practices of our faith as we seek hope and purpose in our
lives? (Or as Frederick says it, "How do we make it possible for people to be theological in their everyday relationships and conversations?")

Over the last decade we have participated in extensive interviews and group conversations about faith development, about
how individuals draw on faith as a resource for living, and about
how the church has nurtured their quest for faithfulness and understanding.

In each congregation, we asked various groups to identify
faithful individuals among their peers—in other words, persons
who have sought to embody faith in their lives and vocations. Then
we invited these individuals to talk about their struggles and stories. Each person we interviewed expressed appreciation for the
church, spoke about the power of the Spirit and of faith in his or
her life, and clarified how the church and others could have been
more helpful at times.

## REFLECTION

*If researchers asked you to identify faithful persons in your congrega-*
*tion, whom would you identify?*

They are ordinary people, found in every congregation, who
simply seek to live faithfully in a broken world, a world where
tears and joy merge, where spirits hunger for relationship and
hope, and where decisions and their results are not always clear.

We all hunger for meaning, for meaningful work, and for a
faith that orients our lives to the spiritual dimension—to God. We
all struggle with questions. We know people who yearn to find
meanings that give life integrity and vitality. Many find their jobs
unsatisfying because they are not able to live out of their deepest
meanings. Others wonder how they can contribute to building a
world of care and nourishment. Still others just try to make it

through another day filled with violence and racism.

We hope that sharing how others have responded to this hunger for meaning and vocation can help all of us to be nourishing presences for the people around us. These stories can help us live with more vitality and faith. For us, speaking with these persons in individual interviews or group conversations has been like Moses standing before the burning bush. We felt we were standing on holy ground as people invited us into faith, meanings, and relationships at the center of their lives.

Some of these ordinary people were well-educated and articulate; others struggled to put their experiences into words. Some had been hurt deeply; others trusted deeply. Many knew they had failed in efforts to be faithful. But above all, they continued seeking to live faithful and committed lives.

The persons we interviewed included high school students, an engineer, an accountant, an educator, an administrator, a social service worker, a communications engineer, a homemaker, a human resources director, a publisher, a lawyer, a young adult in government service, factory workers, a secretary, a service employee, and Vietnamese and German immigrants to the United States. More specifically, we interviewed a woman who worked in the civil rights movement, a man who belonged to the Hitler youth organization as a fifteen-year-old, a young American soldier who witnessed the liberation of a World War II death camp, a couple exploring the call to ordained ministry, a woman who works at a Japanese firm and calls herself a "fundamentalist feminist," a teacher of English for immigrants, a man who travels the world installing cellular phone systems, a man whose life was shattered in the Vietnam War, a homemaker whose avocation is church service, a volunteer for the League of Women Voters, a radiologist, and a stately older woman who played a key role in integrating her Southern congregation. Each seeks to follow a faith tradition and attempts to live with integrity.

# Theology in
# Everyday Lives

We believe that theological reflection—the process of telling one's life story, yearnings, and faith-related questions—is critical for all people. Too often church leaders have assumed that they can impose meanings on which people can base their lives. The Christian tradition, while always in the process of reform, offers truths and wisdom. We find that people draw on that tradition as it fits or seems to speak to their yearnings. But life experiences compel theological reflection. People think about their faith as they need to, and they rely on whatever understanding is available. We have learned that if we do not listen sensitively to others—if we assume we know the meanings people must accept—we risk being irrelevant and ignoring how God's presence reveals itself in their lives.

Therefore, as we participated in these free-flowing conversations, we sought to listen to how faith is critical for meaning making, how people seek to understand their lives in light of these theological convictions, and how theological reflection occurs in everyday life. We have found, like Frederick Buechner, the popular author and theologian, that the stories of lives are theological.

> Our stories are all stories of searching. We search for a good self to be and for good work to do. We search to become human in a world that tempts us always to be less than human or looks to us to be more. We search to love and to be loved. And in a world where it is often hard to believe in much of anything, we search to believe in something holy and beautiful and life-transcending that will give meaning and purpose to the lives we live.[1]

Vocation, temptation, forgiveness, grace, love, holy living, and hope are present in life. The people of God discover and make theological meaning of everyday experiences and define how to carry those meanings into the workplace, home, and community.

The laypersons we interviewed give witness to the power of religious and theological content in their lives. In our book *Educating Christians*, we summarized this process of meaning making and discovery that helps the people of God define their identities as faithful people and live out their vocations of faith in the world:

> As we live, we struggle continually to discover meaning in the midst of disparate events. We find those meanings as we tell stories of our lives and express the beliefs on which we stand. Some experiences draw us deeply into what is called theology—that is, basic questions about the nature of the world, of God, of relationships, of the presence of evil, and of our life commitments. To be human is to dwell in, and live out of, meaning.[2]

The people we interviewed have shown us how actions, questions, searching, vocation, and feelings intermingle. The faith that directs their living is often ambiguous, contradictory, episodic, and imagistic. Stories, practices, and images from their theological traditions sometimes open up the discovery of meaning; at other times they limit and block new insights and revelations. Ordinary events seem to draw us into connecting life and faith. These experiences are occasions to make and discover meaning for living and to discover our identities and vocations.

Let's return to Frederick's struggle with Joy's illness. We asked him how he would change the circumstances of her care if he could. While he wishes for his wife's vitality and joy to be returned, he said that as long as he was able, he would not remove the feeding tube or cease caring for her at home.

> Who knows what purpose this [Joy's illness] is serving? The children, the grandchildren, and great-grandchildren see and hear all of this, and someday they may have to make similar decisions. Maybe what they see and hear

[now] will strengthen them for dealing with that [their own challenges].

Frederick's reflection is filled with the meanings by which he seeks to understand and live with the ambiguity of his wife's coma and a deep love—at the intersection of faith and tears. His conclusion embraces his understanding of vocation, hope, love, care, and living.

A few months later, when we asked Frederick about Joy, he said,

> Well, we almost lost her. Joy acquired pneumonia; therefore, we could have taken the feeding tube out. But before we decided, she rallied. She sure has tenacity about life. I don't know what God wants with Joy, why she is still here. But God must have something in store for her. When I see our grandchildren come in and hold her hand and say, "Hello, Grandma," I believe that God's purpose is to teach them compassion.

Not every person of faith would reach this conclusion, but it has integrity for Frederick and connects with his pain and his understanding of vocation. By speaking his thoughts, Frederick invites conversation, theological and spiritual, that inspires his and others' struggle to find meaning and understanding. He remains steady in the intersection of faith and fear.

## REFLECTION

*Have you ever faced a situation that made no sense to you? How did you search for meaning?*

The persons we interviewed also told us that the church could have assisted them more effectively with this meaning making and discovery. They expressed their wish that the church had helped them more with theological reflection and had better nourished them with the resources of the faith traditions as they sought to live faithfully.

Their words echoed those of theologian John B. Cobb Jr.:

"Theology as the serious activity of faith seeking understanding or self-conscious Christian reflection on important issues has disappeared from many churches." Indeed, in many churches, theology "exists on the periphery, tolerated but not employed in making basic decisions."[3]

How can we all embody the ministry of faithfulness and vocation to which baptism calls us without adequate attention to and assistance from our churches in the reflection necessary to understand our lives as ministry? As The Book of Discipline of The United Methodist Church—2000 states, "Christian ministry is the expression of the mind and mission of Christ by a community of Christians that demonstrates a common life of gratitude and devotion, witness and service, celebration and discipleship. All Christians are called through their baptism to this ministry of servanthood in the world to the glory of God and for human fulfillment."[4] The practices of theological reflection are crucial to living. People seek settings that stimulate spiritual and theological reflection as they struggle to connect life and faith.

## REFLECTION

*What setting has been most helpful to you in dealing with questions of faith? Why?*

Our research confirms that the church cannot simply impose theological patterns or understandings on laypersons. Additionally, laypersons do not draw their theology solely from their faith tradition or from the academic study of theology. For laity, theology emerges from the community of faith as people seek to understand and embody their Christian faith in daily life. Theologians, church leaders, and educators must listen to the people of God as they engage in faithful reflection, or the former group risks becoming irrelevant or even harmful.

The people of God learn the stories, traditions, and practices of their faith community. They draw on these and other experiences, stories, and meanings as they decide, understand, and live their theology. They use natural processes to discover answers to these questions: Who is God? Who am I? What is my relationship to God and the world? What am I called to be and do?

Frederick tries to answer his question about how our lives can be theological in the following words:

> I see life as a journey with a lot of experiences along the way, some good, some bad, some positive, some negative. As I've gone along I've tried to think in terms of what have I accumulated, not in material goods, but in knowledge and wisdom and in experience. You sort of mark your passage by key events in your life. So to me the pilgrimage is just like taking a trip—you're at a beginning and at some time come to your final destination, but along the way it's fascinating.

He adds that the meanings found along the way are emotional, spiritual, and physical as well as intellectual. They are rooted in prayer, in the Bible stories we have learned, in the faith traditions and practices embedded in our consciousness, and in our individual reflection and study. Frederick seeks "confirmation" for the meanings he has found by watching and interpreting signs and by building on the "little insights" that come. It is a process of study, struggle, attention, and prayer.

Frederick so honestly describes the same kind of process used by people in the Bible such as Nicodemus, Paul, or the disciples on the road to Emmaus as they sought to understand and live faithfully. Communities of formation gave each of these persons a tradition, a set of stories and beliefs, and practices and guides to faith. These understandings, deeply embedded, profoundly affected how each person understood and lived.

Life events call forth moments of questioning. For Nicodemus, the event was the presence of an unexpected person (Jesus) who embodied and communicated faith. For Paul, the experience of blindness called into question his vigorous defense of his faith. For the Emmaus disciples, the cause of questioning was the death of their guide and the destruction of hope. In each case, through prayer, experience, searching, insight, and confirmation, these persons eventually found new understandings that gave life meaning and purpose.

At first, Nicodemus the Pharisee watched Jesus from a distance, puzzled and searching. Then he moved to defend Jesus in the midst of his own religious colleagues. Finally he made a claim of faith with his own life as he took care of Jesus' body and risked his reputation in search of truth.

In a parallel way, Paul the Pharisee relied on his faith and defended it against those he saw as a threat to weaken it. However, a profound experience of blindness confronted him with how his faith had blinded him to new options. His life was turned in a new direction. He spread a new gospel.

Finally, the Emmaus disciples, sad and lost, returned home after an apparent failure of hope with the death of Jesus. As they walked and talked, they searched their experiences and the scriptures for meaning and hope. At dinner with a stranger at Emmaus, their hope was resurrected in the breaking of bread. Returning from this transforming event, they became witnesses to the resurrection of hope and new life stemming from their experience of the resurrected Lord Jesus.

## REFLECTION

*Which biblical character is most meaningful for you? How does that person's faith journey shed light on your own journey?*

## Yearnings for God

In the following pages we seek to clarify some yearnings and life concerns that become occasions for theological reflection and faithful living. Join us in the journey to understand this process. As you seek to understand your own life, take advantage of the witness of God acting in the lives of others.

Although this list is not exhaustive, we identified eight areas of yearning in the persons we interviewed:

1. *Yearning for vocation.* In our work and accomplishments we seek for meaning that is consistent with our faith. As Eleanor starkly put it: "I'm just kind of drifting around. Does God just sit up there and say, 'Oh, let's see how far this one can get'? Or am I just not listening?"

2. *Yearning for grace.* We desire to feel God's presence, or as Frederick called it, sense a "confirmation" and "connection to the Holy Spirit." Terri, an adult we interviewed, remembered the moment when at age twelve she first recognized her intimate connection to God: "From that point on, I just began talking to God. I would spend hours and hours before falling asleep at night talking to God about real problems."

3. *Yearning for meaning and healing.* With the illness of a loved one or changes in our own health, we cry out to God for healing and hope. Frederick was doing just that as he sought to understand why Joy continued to suffer and was in a coma. He concluded, "I believe that God's purpose is to teach them [the grandchildren] compassion."

4. *Yearning for justice.* As we see suffering and evil or become aware of the pain and hurt we cause others in the world (our sin), we call on God. Thomas told us of his lifelong quest to make sense of suffering and evil after being sent to Germany as an eighteen-year-old U.S. soldier: "We saw concentration camp victims, which was a terrible experience. It was a very confusing thing, sorting out the suffering we go through and cause others."

5. *Yearning for assurance.* In a world of change and hurt, what can we count on? What can we trust? Bill proclaimed to us, "We really need to lead one another toward God. Someone needs to pick up the standard and start walking."

6. *Yearning for acceptance.* Who am I? Can others accept me? Can I accept myself? Many persons, including Sophia, told us that she hoped to find in the church "a community of people who come, like me, because they are seeking, yearning."

7. *Yearning for new creation.* Experiencing difference often makes us aware of the commitments and values by which we live. Delia told us how she responds to difference. "I will not deny my own experience, because it's real, it's valid! [But we need to] honor other people's experiences too." But even more, we hope for healing of the divisions and the connection of the whole creation in its diversity.

8. *Yearning for hope and for God.* All of the yearnings seem to unite in a cry for connection. The brokenness of relationships makes us cry out. Julia told us that prayer is her resource for hope and vocation. Prayer can renew her hope when all she sees is the "muck out there, and I don't know how to bring a light into it."

Responses to these yearnings give powerful and grace-filled testimony to God's transforming presence. The people we interviewed proclaim that God calls us to enter into life with hope, faith, and risk. Their images communicate the depth of their encounters with God. They see God as a compassionate parent; an ever flowing stream; a life giver; the one who accepts our anger; the one who takes on hurt, weakness, and suffering; the rainbow of many dimensions; the giver of life and joy; the logical one; the forgiving one; the incarnate one; the source of forgiveness and challenge; a miracle worker; and a taproot. Our yearning for God is a yearning for grace, hope, vocation, healing, and meaning in life.

## The Welcome Table

A spiritual written during the time of slavery, when life and hope were daily put at risk, proclaimed:

> I'm going to sit at the welcome table
> Shout my troubles over
> Walk and talk with Jesus
> Tell God how you treat me
> One of these days!

The power of these words reveals that, even in the midst of risk and exploitation, hope can be present.

The Hebrew people and the Christians after them carried forward the dream of a great banquet table set by God where all could receive grace, new life, and nourishment. (See Isa. 25:6-9; 65:17-25; and Luke 14:15-24.) At this table the truth was told of the pain of life and of possibilities of renewal. It was a table of God's new creation.

The persons we interviewed invited us into dialogue around the welcome table of hope and new life, telling the truth of living to one another and seeking to discover how understanding, meaning, and vocation are found and lived. Let's gather around the holy welcome table and listen to the moments when faith is called forth and theological reflection seeks to focus meaning and vocation.

## REFLECTION

Imagine the welcome table Christ sets for you. Who do you envision being there with you? How will the setting feel? What does this image suggest to you about the nature of God? of the church?

# 2

## YEARNING FOR VOCATION

Eleanor's body language revealed the urgency of her questions. Then her blue eyes filled with tears that threatened to spill over.

> I feel right now I have no sense of direction. I don't know what I'm supposed to be doing—that same old question about discernment. I'm just kind of drifting around. Does God just sit up there and say,"Oh, let's see how far this one can get" or am I just not listening? Because I think some people have very clear-cut messages in their lives.

Eleanor was fifty-two years old when she expressed this feeling. Her health had deteriorated so much that she had recently given up her catering business. "Maybe right now my purpose is to rest, and I can't accept that." We humans yearn to know that the way we spend our lives aligns with God's wishes. We yearn for meaningful, faithful work.

The urgency of Eleanor's question resulted from a major shift in vocation. As a young adult, Eleanor actively participated in the civil rights movement at a time when dramatic changes were occurring. She worked for the Urban League. Part of her job was to evaluate historically black colleges that offered programs in allied health. She traveled to fifty-nine of them. She told stories of county sheriffs pounding on her motel room door in the wee hours of the morning to make sure she was not sleeping with her traveling companion, an African-American man. She hid on the floorboard of the car while someone drove hurriedly away from a county that did not appreciate her work for civil rights; gunshots followed. Still, she clearly sensed that she was contributing to something important. During those years Eleanor felt safe even when her situation was rife with danger. Her work was faithful to the commitments of justice and fairness she had inherited from her grandfather.

Now, twenty-five years later, she found herself unable to work. She yearned for a definitive message from God as to how she should use her gifts. Poor health and the loss of a business had left her with "no sense of direction." Neither the earlier end of her marriage nor the death of her mother had left her feeling so uncertain or vulnerable as did this search for work that coincided with her faith. The feeling of protection that accompanied her years of work for justice had evaporated. The yearning for God's guidance had become very pressing in Eleanor's life.

## REFLECTION

*What factors in Eleanor's life contributed to her strong yearning for meaningful work consistent with her faith? What qualities in our families or churches form us as persons who seek to be faithful to God's vision for our lives? Why did Eleanor sense that she was no longer doing what she was "supposed to be doing"?*

## Faith Is Born in Living

Eleanor's childhood did not differ radically from those of many European-American children who grew up during the post-World War II years. Eleanor was raised in a large city in the southeastern United States. "I lived in a walking community. I walked to church

and my lessons. I walked to school. I walked to the grocery store."
School, neighborhood, and church were intertwined. "I took
piano lessons from my choir director," she recalls.

"My parents represented everything of the old South," she told
us. She could identify a "sense of justice and fairness" in her family history. "My paternal grandfather owned a bank when the
Depression hit, and obviously he ended up tail up, as everybody
else did. But he paid back every single person. He worked double
and triple duty because he didn't believe it was fair just to let it
[other people's money] go."

Her grandfather's commitment to justice and fairness was also
part of Eleanor's parents' value system. However, her parents did
not adopt her grandfather's prejudices against persons of color or
Roman Catholics. "I remember asking my mother what happened
to them because they didn't bring forth some of the prejudices
common in that time, and her reply to me was, 'No Christian can
afford those.'" We asked Eleanor if she had any idea where that
statement had come from. She answered, "From a most incredible
faith. She really lived her faith day in and day out. I've never known
her to be judgmental." Eleanor remembered that her mother's faith
was "much like mine in that you were born in it; you grew in it;
you were slowly fertilized." Like many only children, Eleanor was
very close to her parents and grandparents.

One of her earliest memories is of her father giving up his bus
seat in the "for whites only" section to a weary, pregnant African-
American woman. She also recalled her dismay when she discovered that the water fountain marked "colored" had the same kind
of water as the other fountain labeled "white." She had expected it
to be red or blue or some other "color." Her family taught her to
care about justice and fairness for all people.

Eleanor and her parents always belonged to a Methodist congregation. She told us proudly that her parents encouraged her
friendship with girls from different cultural and faith traditions.
One friend was Greek Orthodox. Another was Jewish. Eleanor vis-

ited in the homes of her friends and took part in their religious practices. As a young girl, Eleanor did not realize that such openness to religious and cultural differences was unusual. In retrospect, Eleanor is pleased that her parents allowed her exposure to the practices of other faiths.

## REFLECTION

*What stories do you remember about your parents that illustrate their commitment to fairness or openness to difference? What differences did you observe between your parents' and grandparents' values? How did your parents explain those differences to you?*

Giving was another value that Eleanor's parents and the culture reinforced. "In my Southern context, we are taught from day one to give, to give, to give, to give. Then we come into the church and we are hit with another kind of giving—your time, your talents, your money, and all that other kind of stuff, and there is this constant outward flow going on." Eleanor remembers her mother volunteering twice a week to read to the children at a preschool that served low-income families, and she remembers going with her mom. The model of giving to others was powerful. Giving was entwined with religion for Eleanor. "I get a more religious feeling when I can do things for people," she commented.

In Eleanor's family, giving was tempered with self-reliance. "You just did not rely on people for things that you could do for yourself. You would get up and do it!" Eleanor realized that her family's emphasis on giving to others and being self-reliant made it difficult for her to accept help or receive anything she had not earned. "The church does not teach us to receive. If I have trouble taking from you, goodness gracious, the trouble I have taking from God!" Eleanor acknowledged that God's gift of salvation through the life, death, and resurrection of Jesus made her ask, "Why am I worthy?" She admits that this question has bothered her all of her life.

## REFLECTION

*What was said about giving in your family? Do you recall any times when your family received gifts that were difficult to receive? Do you ever find it difficult to believe that you are worthy of God's love? How do you reconcile the need to be self-reliant with the need to accept the grace of God's love?*

Eleanor describes the time of her childhood as a time of "normalcy." Nurtured by a homogeneous neighborhood with Protestant, North American cultural values, and a close family, Eleanor felt safe. Both her parents and the culture in which they lived taught her to be fair, to live her faith, to welcome difference, to give to others, to be self-reliant, and to be a good citizen at church and school.

The period of college and young adulthood began to challenge some values Eleanor had taken for granted, but this process took place in the relative safety of a university and church in her hometown. She encountered a larger world of both people and values. "Life just kinda begins to open up for you about that age," she remarked. A college professor challenged her faith in a Bible class she refers to as Heresy 101. "Most of us walked in with child faith. You just accept what was taught to you. [This professor] just egged you [on]; he would just sit there and prod you. So that was the first rattling that occurred." Eleanor took two religion courses in addition to the required class. She remembers extensive verbal exchanges with the controversial professor and that his questions "rattled" the assumptions she had inherited.

At the same time that this professor challenged her faith assumptions, Eleanor participated in a group at church. She describes it like this: "The leader of the college group was just a fantastically wonderful person. He had this off-the-wall sense of humor; he was intellectually challenging; and he would ask the other side of the questions that you never had asked before, so it was fun." Although Eleanor attended college in the same town where she grew up, she became part of two settings that challenged her faith intellectually. One was threatening (the classroom) while the other was nurturing (the church group). College was a fertile and exhilarating time of exploring while still safely near her parents.

"As I look back, it was a fermenting time. I lived on the campus, but I took my laundry home. I went to eat with my grandparents once a week. The umbilical [cord] wasn't totally cut." She was still doing what she was "supposed to do" as she encountered the new ideas within the context of the university. Eleanor had not yet endured any life event that made her feel outside the protection of God or her family.

## REFLECTION

*What happened to your faith and values as you began the process of leaving home and entering adulthood? Recall mentors who were especially helpful. How did they encourage or challenge you?*

## Living Our Faith Commitments

In the relative safety of nearby family, Eleanor began to live out the justice and fairness commitments her family had taught. The university's tentative efforts at racial integration caused a furor on campus and in the community. Eleanor recalls how meetings of students brought up "issues [such as] could we sit on the same toilet and on and on." Eleanor was beginning to see the inconsistencies in how the culture treated persons of color, and she spoke out. "All these Africans were on campus who had been there when I got there, and I raised my hand in the middle of a meeting and asked why they thought we were desegregating when we had all these African students on campus?" She could see the disparity between the treatment of international students and African-American students. "And I was point-blank told it was because they 'didn't count!' That's the way I grew up—with those kinds of stupid answers to issues!" She got in trouble again for offering to share her umbrella:

> I was coming down the quad, and one of the black women came out of the library. It was one of those Southern storms that come up suddenly. I happened to have an umbrella. We were both going to the cafeteria, so I said, "Why don't we share it?" Seems like a logical thing. Two people out in the rain, one umbrella—you get under it. I got called before house council (on which I sat) because I had done this.

For Eleanor, the university years provided an opportunity to test her inherited traditions and values against predominant cultural values. Her parents' loving and just examples helped equip her to resist the injustices of the culture. She felt confident that she was doing what she was "supposed to do," and she experienced little doubt or fear as she challenged the prejudices and injustices of "the system."

## REFLECTION

*Psychological theories of human development identify adolescence and young adulthood as periods when we test the values inherited from our families and claim the values we will adopt as adults. Remember a time when you tested or stood up for inherited values. Remember key mentors or teachers who provided a safe place for you to challenge values.*

Eleanor reported that she did what her *Father Knows Best* culture expected when she graduated from college—she married and had a child. She taught school for a couple years. She was doing what she was "supposed to do." But the marriage was difficult and did not last. For the sake of her child, she knew she must end the marriage. Her parents supported her decision. Although her culture and her church did not readily accept single mothers, Eleanor managed to make a place for herself. She even served as an advocate for a singles ministry in her congregation and succeeded in changing some attitudes.

"Then I ended up in the civil rights movement for seventeen years." She told of this move to justice work with little fanfare, but it was a huge shift from the culturally imposed expectations for young women at that time. She said she was just looking for a summer job until school started up again, but civil rights became her vocation for seventeen years.

## REFLECTION

*When has your life taken a huge turn without your intending it? How did it happen? When did you realize what the change meant? How do you see God in connection with this change?*

Eleanor's work with the Urban League was full of surprises. She remembers this time in her life as one of "exhilarating fatigue":

> I mean, it was the most unbelievable experience of my life, walking in there. The way I grew up, I met the housekeepers or the yard people. I had never met peer-level blacks, and here were people who had doctorates and master's degrees. So I go into this agency, and they all wear coats and ties, and they speak like I do. My boss took me—spent three days and we toured the city—to the other part of the city [where the African-American community was]. This was kind of a cultural thing we were taught: You didn't go there. It was the first time I really remember being white. They spent a lot of time acculturating me, but it was done with a great deal of care. It was their desire to share their community with me.

Gaining acceptance in the African-American culture and in the community of people who worked for civil rights and justice was both exhilarating and exhausting.. Eleanor remembers, "I was on a high a lot of that period of time." She learned a great deal about herself as she discovered her "whiteness" and privileges she had taken for granted that were denied others. "It was probably the most content professional life I ever had. It was one time I knew I was doing what I was supposed to be doing."

Eleanor's work with the Urban League clashed with the prevailing cultural values of the white South. Her decision to seek a graduate degree in sociology from a historically black university put her in conflict with her beloved grandfather. Eleanor wanted to attend this university so she could learn sociology from professors who would challenge the interpretations of the dominant culture. Yet she was a single mother with a full-time (difficult and sometimes dangerous) job and going to graduate school at night. Her parents agreed to help with child care, but they asked her to inform her grandparents of her decision. She recalls:

> I'll never forget this to my dying day: My grandfather called me and said, "Tell me what it is you wanted to go to this school for." And I said, "I want to get a master's degree. I want to do some research." And he said, "Pick any school in the world. I will pay your salary you're making now. I will pay for the housekeeper to take care of your child. I will pay your tuition." I mean it was a total free ride, and I said, "No. It's important that I stay here and do this." He accepted that [decision] from me and that [his acceptance] was a great gift, but he opened his wallet and he took out a one-hundred-dollar bill, which was a big bill at that time. He said, "Keep this in your wallet. Maybe if you run into trouble you can buy your way out." I kept it through my whole two years in grad school, and I walked back in when I graduated and handed it to him.

Fueled by her resolve, Eleanor traveled many evenings from her middle-class white neighborhood to an African-American neighborhood and a campus where she was one of only a few white students. The values of justice, fairness, and self-reliance her grandfather had modeled were the same values that enabled Eleanor to take this stand. When asked what had given her the strength to stand up to her grandfather, Eleanor replied, "Two things: One is his love for me—I knew how great that was. And I felt so comfortable in that decision. I knew it was right, and I knew God had his hand in that."

## REFLECTION

*Recall a time when you had to stand up to your parents or another family member for a decision you believed in deeply. Did you express that decision in theological terms? If not, would you today?*

Even in her decision to attend a university that most of her family and friends would not even visit, Eleanor's sense of doing what she "was supposed to be doing" meant that she felt God's protection. The night that Dr. Martin Luther King Jr. was assassinated, she was nearly trapped by fires and angry crowds, but two students at the university led her to safety. "I was just so amazed at what had happened to me. Again it is a part of that 'protection.' I felt God was taking care of me." Eleanor went on to say that she probably would not have acknowledged God's hand in it at that time, but looking back, God's presence is clear to her.

Learning to be part of the African-American community was painful at times. "I guess the hardest part was being distrusted initially when I carried trust in my heart. I wish people could just know this, but it doesn't work that way. I've never really had much trouble once people got to know me . . . but you hear the accent, you see the blue-eyed blonde, you just kind of wonder. . . ." Still, the common values of the people working at the Urban League bonded them together. "Almost every person that I worked with up there was active in a local church—primarily Baptist, but African Methodist Episcopal also—and I think that makes a difference in any approach to life. So they were very nurturing to me."

## REFLECTION

*Entering a new community often teaches us to see the world in a new way. When have you experienced such stretching? Who mentored you in the new setting?*

All this time Eleanor was raising a son. They attended Sunday school in the church where her family members were still active. She taught him to love books and learning. At the time of her interview, Eleanor's son had just completed a Ph.D. and was a full-time dad caring for an infant daughter while his wife pursued her career. Describing her son, Eleanor said,

> He is wonderful! I tried very hard to teach him to be open to people, and I look back at his groomsmen—his best man was black; the next one was Jewish—so I think I succeeded in that regard. He has a terrific sense of humor. I know I will always be his mother and he will always be my son, but we're friends. We're at that level, and that's neat.

Her love for and commitment to her family were evident. Eleanor glowed as she talked about her son. His continued commitment to justice and fairness—values at the center of Eleanor's life—indicated to her that she had done a good job as a parent; she had done what she was "supposed to do." She was able to be a parent, a graduate student, and a worker in the civil rights movement. She had enough energy to do a good job in all these arenas.

## REFLECTION

*Identify times in your life when you had enough energy to do several tasks because you knew that doing them all was right and good. How* did you understand that work in relation to God's will for your life? What did you think you were "supposed to do"?

Although Eleanor remained active in the church through all these years, she felt a discontinuity between her work for civil rights and her church life. "I came to the church and it was white, and I left and went back to my integrated world." She chose not to talk about her "integrated world" in the church. "It was just easier not to. I don't know how to talk about that time or our work." She feared sounding "sanctimonious," so she did not speak of her work for justice. Thus the distinction between her "religion" and her church became important to Eleanor. "My trouble is primarily finding a community where I can share my religion." She clarifies, "My being out there and doing what I did was my religion, and I think that's because I knew it was what I was supposed to be doing."

## REFLECTION

Which, if any, of your values are inconsistent with those of your faith community? How do you reconcile that discord? If you shared your values with your faith community, how do you predict they would respond?

After seventeen years of this "exhilarating fatigue"—experiencing danger and challenge, being a single parent, and surviving on three or four hours of sleep a night—Eleanor found herself having headaches, not wanting to go to work, not having the cheerleading attitude.

> We had kind of an open-style management system in the office. The boss was pretty open to discussion and tugging at things. I realized I didn't care about those discussions, those kinds of things, and if I did care about them, [my concern] was always negative. Leaving it [the Urban League] was the hardest part in terms of my religious convictions, because I felt like I belonged there. I wasn't sure

it was the right thing to do. I didn't get any clear-cut answers, so I went with my hunch.

<u>REFLECTION</u>

*Think of a time when you made a change in your life. What signals did
you listen to for guidance? What physical clues pointed to the need for
change? Did you receive any signals from other people? How did God's
guidance affect your decision making?*

The lack of a clear sign was mitigated by an opportunity that
Eleanor calls "almost too convenient." She went to work in a
friend's shop. "I thought, *Well, maybe this is what I'm supposed to be
doing.*" However, neither her work with the friend nor the catering
business that Eleanor opened on her own satisfied her as much as
her earlier work with the Urban League. As Eleanor talked about
these years, her voice took on tones of failure and sadness. The urgency of her need to be faithful to "what I am supposed to do"
and the lack of energy or direction left her saying, "I feel right now
I have no sense of direction. I don't know what I'm supposed to
be doing."

## Vocation As Knowing What You Are Supposed to Do

Knowing that she is doing what she is supposed to do seems to be
Eleanor's deepest desire, but this certainty eluded her in the period
following her civil rights work. Her health began to deteriorate.
Finally, unable to continue the catering business on her own, she
closed it and searched for a new way to make a living. She really
struggled with this search, battling pain and fatigue as she fought
to figure out what the next phase of her life should be. "Maybe
right now my purpose is to rest, but I can't accept that," she explained. The uncertainty and yearning for meaningful work had

challenged her sense of purpose. Eleanor confessed that she "had no clue" about what she should do. She yearned to know whether God approved of her life.

> We measure everything in our society. You go through grammar school and you get report cards. You do the same thing in high school. You get on the job and you have performance reviews. Then you have every talk show in the world putting out standards for married life, or you go off to Marriage Encounter [a marriage enrichment seminar] and they tell you how you ought to be doing. There is feedback constantly. Where you don't have a report card is with God. The biggest one of all, and there is no clue! Have I done enough? I don't have any idea. [We asked, "Enough for what?" She replied, "Eternal life."] You know, they don't say anywhere if 50 percent or 60 percent is enough. Nothing that we hold onto and understand is used to measure whether we have pleased God, which is, I guess, why they call it faith, but it's still very disconcerting to me not to have some handles.

In the midst of this urgent yearning for clarity about God's will for her life and for God's approval, Eleanor could still affirm her sense of God's presence. We asked, "Do you still feel those hands that hold you up?" She replied, "Sometimes I don't even ask and they just come. Like your mom used to hold you. Sometimes I feel like that. It's that very secure feeling that you get." She recalled the terrible time when her mother was dying of cancer. "I know God was there, and I'm very grateful for that. It's funny. When we were being shot at or in these very high peaks of crisis, God never failed. I have failed miserably at times, but God has never failed."

A recent trip to the dentist had provided a powerful vision that Eleanor understood as an experience of God's presence.

I'm lying there and I can't quite control the line between cognizance and drifting over, and all of a sudden God was there. I mean [God] was right in my face! God took a knife and just pulled my flesh back and let me see inside. I was so disgusted by what I saw—not the organs but the un-cleanness. I burst into tears. And God patched me back up and said, "What are you going to do?"

Although this image obviously upset her, Eleanor described God as "so much love." She said she wished God had been clearer about "which part [of her] is so bad."

### REFLECTION

*Recall any times when you dreamed of God or had a vision that you understood to be from God. What was the message for you? Have you found places to share the dream or vision? Why or why not?*

Returning to our question, "What is the purpose of life?" Eleanor wondered aloud if perhaps eternal life is that purpose. "Having enjoyed God's company in this life, if that's [God's company] what I get for eternity, that would be nice." In another setting, Eleanor commented, "I know less about God now than I did [as a young adult], but I experience God on a far deeper level than I did then." She described these experiences of God as "an incredible peace, but it doesn't mean the whole world stops or the chaos in my life stops or anything. It means I can face it and I can get through it, that kind of thing. I'm not in charge. Somebody else is, and I don't have to worry."

Eleanor could point to repeated experiences of God's presence, yet she wanted something more. She commented, "Maybe my whole problem is jumping over the abyss from the cognitive to faith. Maybe I'm just a slow learner." She continued the urgent quest by regularly participating in an intensive Bible study along with other opportunities for teaching and learning. She read widely.

In spite of Eleanor's experiences of the holy and her constant study, she could not find peace about her life. Restless and dissatisfied, she needed not only to be clear about vocation but also to know that this was what she was "supposed to do" from God's point of view. Studying the text of Eleanor's interview, we were struck by how often she repeated the phrase "supposed to do." Eleanor urgently wanted to know that God approved of what she was doing and to regain the sense of God's protection she had had during the Urban League years.

Maybe Eleanor tries to obey God to earn God's acceptance, in the same way that she obeyed her family, school, and church as a girl and felt safe and protected. During her years in the Urban League, she felt obedient to God's will for justice, and she felt safe and protected. Now her uncertainty about whether she remains obedient has left her feeling unprotected. Failing health and energy exacerbated the feelings of vulnerability. "I want to be sure that I'm doing what I'm supposed to do!" Eleanor declared. But perhaps most of all she wanted to feel assured of God's protection.

## Yearning for Vocation

This yearning was powerfully present in Eleanor's interview, but it was also a recurring theme in many other interviews. Claude, a middle-aged man who served as an active volunteer in youth ministry, commented that he knew what he was supposed to do by affirmation he received from the youth. "I talked with a lot of youth after the night I got up and shared my story, and it just reinforced my feeling that God is calling me to take my experiences in life and go into youth ministry." At the time of Claude's interview, his church had just asked him to find a different place to volunteer. This request challenged his assurance of obedience to God's call, and he was deeply troubled.

In chapter 1 we mentioned Frederick's search for what he

called "confirmation." He told several stories of times of confirmation. One was about his Sunday school class.

> I see life as a journey with a lot of experiences along the way, some positive, some negative. I've tried to think of what I have accumulated in wisdom and experience. I remember teaching the young couples class here. We were talking about the meaning of sabbath. We had an excellent discussion. I went home, and I can remember the spot: I was in the hallway thinking about the lesson, and all of a sudden a great warmth came over me. It was just like a great rush or something. In trying to put a label on that experience, it seemed that I got a sort of an endorsement that we were on the right track with that discussion.

Frederick identified these incidents of "confirmation" as important assurances that he was doing what he was supposed to do. He even remembered a time when he had felt sure that "I would see confirmation signs that would establish the truth of these things." He looked confidently for signs of confirmation through the rest of his life.

### REFLECTION

*What sort of signals or confirmations do you expect as guidance for your life? From what or whom do you expect them to come? What expectations do you have for guidance from God?*

A young man who worked as a mathematician for a computer firm also yearned for meaningful work consistent with his faith. Gary said, "I know my gift [for mathematics] is from God. I want to find out how I can work at Comp USA and live my life as a Christian in the best way. I'm struggling with how my job calls me to be a profit prophet."

Some persons, like Bill, find careers that easily fit with their commitment. Bill had always loved science and found himself drawn to research as an undergraduate. His specialty in chemical engineering led him to a position with a large corporation that deals with recycling and environmental protection. "If you really believe that this is God's creation and that part of our responsibility is to take care of God's creation, then my job is a satisfying fit." Bill's work and his faith were congruent.

Franz told us that he had struggled for many years before "it finally dawned on me that what the Lord wants us to do is to do ministry in all of life. It relieves tension to put things in the right order: God first, others next, and me after that." At sixty-six, Franz had found some peace in regard to his yearning for meaningful work consistent with his faith. He felt confident about his life priorities. But more often the people we spoke with were like Eleanor or Sheryl, who said, "I think that I feel like there is something I'm being called to do, but I don't know what it is. I do know that I'm not prepared."

Twenty-nine-year-old Christine was on a definite vocational track and was experiencing success. An environmental engineer with a degree from Massachusetts Institute of Technology, her work aligned with her values of protecting the environment. "Being an environmentalist is part of who I am," she reported. But she was restless, seeking a way to focus more on relationships with people and to be less tied to a computer. So, she said, "I started questioning whether I should get out of science, what I should do. I went to my Disciple Bible Study group with the questions: Do I want to be a minister? Do I want to quit being an environmental engineer? I didn't come out with an answer. Or maybe I did in the fact that I'm still an environmental engineer," she said with a rueful smile. Like Eleanor, Christine sought meaningful work consistent with her faith and values.

## Believers and the Church

The people of God seek to be faithful and yearn to live in ways that will be acceptable to God. This is a theological and spiritual task. We learned values from our families and the communities where we grew up. But many of us move beyond those values, claiming some and tossing others aside. Eleanor retained the value of justice and fairness but extended it to people unlike her. We may act on those values in spite of disapproval from family or culture. Yet, we yearn for God's approval. Some seek signs from God. Others work it out more logically. But those who love God yearn to respond faithfully to God's love with their whole lives. We yearn to find meaningful work that is consistent with our faith.

### REFLECTION

*How do you experience the yearning for a vocation that aligns with your faith? How does your current work coincide with your faith? In what ways do you look for "a confirmation" as Frederick does? How has God communicated with you about your vocation?*

A profound theological tension exists in this yearning for vocation. Our faith tells us that God is active in the creation, in human living. It also tells us that God has purposes for creation and that we are accepted, called, sent, and empowered as God's witnesses. Furthermore, we carry God's mission and love into the world. Nevertheless, our faith also tells us that God accepts us as God's children; we are adopted as heirs of the kingdom. Therefore, even if we are weak and vulnerable, even if we become unable to continue to carry out the mission, God still accepts us.

We live in a culture of work, success, and accomplishment. These worldly values often infect even the deepest commitments and understandings of the faith. We begin to think that our work becomes the primary measure of our value. We easily come to feel unworthy and wasted. We forget that vocation is a response to God's initial action of loving, forgiving, and claiming us. God's love calls us to respond in gratitude and to engage lovingly and passionately in God's mission in the world. At least from the perspective of the greater faith tradition, Eleanor was right when she asked, "What is God asking of me now? Perhaps God is calling me to wait." Perhaps God calls us to recognize the deep love and care that God gives even when we are not as strong and as powerful as we once were. Perhaps we misunderstand the nature of God's protection as well as the nature of our value in God's eyes.

The search for vocation can powerfully motivate theological reflection and faithful living. However, it must be held in tension with the grace of God's ever-flowing love and acceptance of "even the least of these." Both grace and vocation comprise a part of faith. The tension between them in our lives powerfully motivates theological reflection. It is not our works that make us valuable; what gives us value is the fact that God created us and accepts us. Too often we seek to make life meaningful through our works rather than through living graciously in God's presence and in God's world where we are called to contribute and serve.

Eleanor's urgent question needs a place to be recognized and accepted. She has never felt free to share her justice work with her church. So how can she process the questions now?

## REFLECTION

*In what ways does your congregation explicitly affirm the value of all persons? of all ages? of all abilities? of all social classes? of all races and nationalities? In what areas does your church not affirm the value of all persons?*

# 3

## YEARNING FOR GRACE

Many commentators have described the United States as a place where people "live to work." Strangers meeting for the first time often define themselves in terms of what they do. This preoccupation with work and accomplishment, unfortunately, diverts our understanding of vocation. Instead of understanding living as a grateful response to the grace of God, we rely on accomplishments (works) to provide the meaning and purpose for our lives. In the last chapter we saw the tensions between works and grace. A key yearning for the persons with whom we talked was to seek for and to understand the gracious presence of a living God.

Remember that Frederick was a bit embarrassed to speak about his feeling of being connected to the Holy Spirit. His sense of connection enables him to approach life with a great deal of openness and trust.

Eleanor's quest to renew the feeling of grace probably focuses her search to reclaim the sense of vocation she had earlier in her life. As she described strangers who helped her on the night her city was burning, she spoke of feeling protected and encircled. She talked about feeling protected and encircled during the harrowing days of voter registration when some persons intended to harm her. No longer certain about her connection with God, she seeks meaning and vocation. Eleanor hopes and prays that with a new vocational clarity, she will recover the sense of purpose and protection.

Many great Christian leaders experienced this same search. Martin Luther wrote about his efforts to fulfill all of the laws and expectations. But his best efforts never gave him the connection to grace that we find in Paul's letters. Paul experienced the reality of being saved by grace alone. John Wesley also begged for the certainty that God's grace was available to him. He fervently wished to possess the simple faith of the Moravians whom he encountered while traveling back to England from the New World. God's grace seemed an ever-present reality to them. Wesley hungered for this reality until the night of his heartwarming experience when God's grace claimed him. His method, the method of discipleship that gave birth to Methodism, was a response to grace.

John Newton, a former slave trader, wrote the great hymn "Amazing Grace" to express his regret and prayers for forgiveness. Yet, new life had become a reality for him. His life had been transformed, and he sought forgiveness from those he had harmed. Amazing grace relieved his fears and guided him in new ways of living and efforts to repay those he had wronged.

> Through many dangers, toils, and snares,
> I have already come;
> 'tis grace hath brought me safe thus far,
> and grace will lead me home.

The search for this amazing grace, for connection to and acceptance by God, is a crucial yearning of persons of faith.

## Come with Your Oil and Wine

Julia teaches English as a Second Language to women. She takes seriously the vocation of a teacher. She endeavors to connect deeply with the lives of her students, feeling that literacy training has brought her and her students together "as human beings." Through literacy she hopes to help protect these women from becoming victims of unscrupulous people in the wider society. She knows they are vulnerable, and she wants to help them develop skills that will enable them to shape their own lives. As she teaches them to speak and to read English, Julia engages her students in talking deeply about the things that matter most and then about their needs. She does not simply treat these discussions as classroom assignments. When she learns of needs, she gets involved. She shares her faith and seeks to help the women find job contacts.

Julia's sense of vocation is clear. She describes the call of the Christian gospel as going "right out into the people. I think we have to do just what the apostles did. We have to essentially go and be with the people. And that might not be easy." Realizing the grandness of her vision, she asks, "How can we live for God and for others?" She understands that God has called her to encourage people and to risk for others. Her motto of living comes from Mother Teresa: "I don't do great things. I do small things with great love."

Almost in an embarrassed tone, Julia ended our conversation by thanking us for caring "about an ordinary life." Then she described herself and the power of grace in her life:

> You know what I've discovered? and you probably have too—There actually isn't an ordinary life. Everyone is special. That's weird. It's one of those paradoxes that you always run into with faith. It's the most simple, but it's the most profound. It's the most common, and it's the most eloquent. That's one of the most wonderful things about God: [God is] the beginning and the end. [God is] the complex and the simple. The near and the far. The in and the out. God is the source of life. God is the grace that fills life and sends one graciously to risk for others.

Julia used the images of communication and relationship to speak of God—"completing, fulfilling, at-one-ment, atonement." The feeling of being at one with God, of being deeply connected to God, is important to her. Yet she volunteered that she doesn't feel that she adequately fulfills her call. She is always challenged to be more faithful.

## REFLECTION

*What image would you choose to describe the connection God desires with humans? A scripture passage or hymn may provide an image, or you may think of one of your own. What kind of connection would you like to have with God?*

Julia tells of a profound shift that occurred in her life when the question "Who am I?" with all the related concerns with self-image was overcome by a new question: "Whose am I?" In other words, she began living by grace instead of by her own efforts.

> Now "Whose I am" is good. I don't quite know how [this shift] happened. But I think I've come through that, by God's grace. "Whose am I?" I am my heavenly Father's child. I am a person who has fallen many times, but [God] still loves me. I belong to God; God made me. I am forgiven. God knows everything about me and still claims me; God still welcomes me back. I have closed the door, and God persisted in knocking.

What a powerful expression of grace! This expression was not born of ease and good gifts. For years, Julia's life seemed primarily concerned with pleasing others and living by their agendas. She experienced times of risk and rebellion as well as times of tremendous loneliness. But at the heart of all of these feelings was a search for connection, mystery, and transcendence. When she was a child, her mother served as a member of the altar guild. Julia observed a sacredness as her mother laid out the priest's vestments on the vesting table, accompanying each one with a special prayer and putting it in a special place. Her actions symbolized preparation for "putting on Christ." Julia recalled, "She acted differently and made me act differently." The sense of sacredness and of new life permeated Julia's consciousness and served as the foundation for her continuing search for God and for faithfulness, even when she broke many rules.

> Before I could ask theological questions, I saw modeled for me faithfulness, unquestioning worth. . . . I love the music and the mystery of the church. I remember sitting there for all-night vigils on Holy Thursday. And the wind in the old building and how the building creaked like it was alive. You could just hear the timbers, like some big creature. And the building was all dark.

The sense of mystery and the experience of unquestioning worth pursued her. Nevertheless, hurt accumulated from the losses. Julia recalls, "I had tried living without God and doing my variety of picking and choosing. And it never worked."

After eighteen months of immense crisis, during which her mother died, her daughter angrily moved away from home, her best friend was murdered, and another friend refused to any longer be her rock, Julia was almost crushed. Life hit her with crises of meaning, illness, violence, and death. Slowly she rediscovered her dependence on God. She describes this time:

> That's God's way of bringing you through. You have to admit that you hurt. Sometimes God asks you, "How far are you going to get from me before you won't come back? How far will you go before you shipwreck?" . . . That's what happens in your faith if you don't talk to God, if you don't praise or thank God. Even when you're hurting, if you don't sing to God and let God sing to you,

pretty soon there is nothing left. I had to be honest. I had to let God know the worst thing, from down deep in here [pointing to her heart] where I didn't think I could go. I had to let God know my pain. I said: "How much more, please? I'm ripped open. Here it is: everything that is hurting, right in front of you. Please heal my pain. Please, God. Come with your oil and your wine and pour it on me because I need to be healed."

Julia's prayers and laments revealed the depth of her pain—a depth so painful that she did not know if she could touch it. Yet, in her case, and in her life, that sacred presence of grace became real. Theological reflection meant drawing on all of the stories, practices, and beliefs of her childhood. The commitments and friendships of her community of faith also offered support and care. But a moment of grace claimed Julia and sent her on a journey that has resulted in a lifetime of small, faithful actions.

She describes the way she connected everyday thinking and her theological convictions so she could understand the power of grace in her life and the willingness of God to accept her.

I remember that summer. We'd had two years of drought. Everything was dry. I just hit the point where I was going through a menopausal beginning. My body was drying up. My eyes felt dry. And I can remember looking out the front window. There wasn't any green anymore. The summer sun had beaten the ground to death. The ground was like cement. I thought, "God, what in the world has happened that I feel like you are nowhere? Everything has been pulled away. Where are you?"

And there was a Sunday morning I was asked to teach Sunday school, and I volunteered. That morning my husband was out pulling weeds. Only weeds were living in our yard. They were tough, like iron. He took and pulled one. He kept pulling and pulling . . . and there was the root, with a tiny bit of green, down deep where it had found the moisture it craved. He brought it to me as I was getting ready for church. He said, "Look at this thing. Look what I brought up." I looked at it; I looked at this plant and knew it was going to survive. It was right out by the road where the sun baked the soil. There had been no water out there for who knows how long. And it was an ugly little plant, almost gray. As I looked at it, I thought, "My God, that's me. You've done it, Lord; you're here!" I had held on long enough. I knew with God's help, I would survive.

The gift of insight, this experience of grace itself, had to be interpreted. New life became a transforming reality even though the pain of loss and hurt still was present. Julia missed those who had meant so much to her, but now life focused on the question, "Whose am I?"

## REFLECTION

*Recall a time when you felt really low or overwhelmed. What lifted you out of the depth? Did you experience any sign that life would get better?*

# Searching for and Responding to Grace

Grace lies at the heart of faith. Grace gives us the strength to face our losses, calls us to new life, and connects us to God. Life is God's gift of grace. Several persons we interviewed spoke of discovering the power of God's grace as children.

Lan, a Vietnamese immigrant to the United States, told us about growing up in French-occupied Vietnam. Even at an early age, she felt sinful and unworthy—probably in part a result of colonialism. She says that her mother taught her how to behave, but she never could live up to her mother's expectations.

However, the sounds of the services of a small Catholic mission church reached out of the building into the streets. As Lan passed the church, she heard "beautiful music." She heard the priest speaking about the love and acceptance of Jesus Christ. She often sat on the steps and listened to the stories of this Jesus who accepted persons who were different and excluded. But more than hearing the words, she watched the attitude and acceptance of the priest. He incarnated the love of Jesus in his life, modeling love and acceptance. For her, this stranger modeled grace.

Lan asked her mother about Jesus. Her mother, a devout Buddhist, told her that she did not know about Jesus but would go with her to the church to find out. Mother and daughter experienced firsthand this love and acceptance about which the priest spoke. She says, "They [the priest and the nuns] proved their love by their living." Moreover, she talks about listening to the music and experiencing the sacredness of the holy space.

> I went there for quiet. Early on, I didn't know how to pray, so I just sat there. And then the peace would come. When I went home, it was like I had been emptied of everything [of worries, of feelings of sinfulness, of hurt]. God showed me. The time I spent in silence there was really fantastic. I couldn't understand it then; now I understand.

The idea of emptying connected well to Vietnamese Buddhist tradition. Emptying oneself of anything that separated one from God was a deep belief. Through her experience of emptying, Lan heard God and knew God accepted her. She dealt with many abuses during the last years of the Vietnam War, including the loss of her husband and her own narrow escape from death. Lan credits her survival of this difficult time to the love and acceptance she received from her family and from the priests and nuns, as well as her powerful experience of the presence of God in Jesus. For her the cross of Jesus and the suffering of Mary exemplify how new life is born from loss and suffering. Jesus and Mary are models that help her begin to understand her own suffering.

Today Lan responds to this love and acceptance through serving others. Each week she goes to her church, discovers the names of persons in need, and prays in the sanctuary, sometimes for hours, for God's grace and healing in the various situations. She says, "So many miracles happen in my life." She returns these blessings through her actions. Another way she ministers is to sit in the waiting rooms of hospital emergency rooms. When she feels that someone needs care and support, she approaches that person and asks if she can pray with him or her. Her ministry of prayer and presence offers acceptance, love, grace, and hope. Lan's ministry is a response to the grace she has experienced.

Terri also tells about a powerful childhood experience. All of the talk about God she heard at church seemed so distant and foreign. Going to church was a stuffy and boring experience for her. Yet, one evening, after a session of confirmation class on the personal character of God, a thought startled Terri: *If that's a person up there and I'm falling asleep, God must be falling asleep too!* While this is obviously an anthropomorphic image of God shaped by a childish mind, that image influenced her from then on. She says, "I just began talking to God. I would spend hours before falling asleep at night talking to God about real problems." For her, God's grace invited her into relationship. God has been accessible and has guided her. Both her life and service to others are gracious responses to this love and acceptance.

## REFLECTION

*What experiences of God did you have as a child? How do those experiences shape your faith today?*

# In the Deepest
# Moments of Loss

Wilma, a retired university administrator, broke barriers for other women in her career. Early in the women's movement, she and another colleague invited young women into a support group to help them understand their calls to service and their unique gifts for leadership and community. Late in life, Wilma married her soul mate. He supported her career, and they nurtured each other's lives. At the end of worship services in their church, Wilma and her spouse reached out to visitors, offering hospitality and helping the visitors connect with members.

Wilma grew up in a pastor's home. Her mother's painful death from cancer when Wilma was only five left her father a widower with four children to raise. She describes her father as a supportive and welcoming presence who faced loss, hardship, and challenge with confidence in God's grace. In spite of two fires that destroyed his home and despite threats to his life, he courageously worked for racial justice and against mob violence during a risky time in his community when a black man was accused of rape. Wilma remembers asking her father, "How could God let this happen to a minister, to lose your house twice [both through fires, one of them arson] and have my mother die?" While she doesn't remember his reply, she knows he helped her understand that "we don't always have the answers" and that "God didn't prevent bad things from happening to good people." Through her father she experienced God's love and grace and knew they were real.

She tells a delightful story about how her father broke with tradition to share grace and offer options to his children. Her older sister loved to dance. She adds, "Methodist ministers' kids didn't dance back in those days. One of the things my dad did says a lot about his understanding. When she [my sister] wanted to go to her high school dance, he took her out to buy her first formal and let her go to the dance." In turn, he supported Wilma's decision, after college, during a time when single women usually did not leave home, to move to Washington, D.C., live in a boardinghouse with friends, and begin a career.

Cancer and death have dogged Wilma and her family. As mentioned previously, she was only five when her mother died. When she was about forty, several people in her family died from cancer—her brother, an uncle, and then one sister and a sister's husband within five weeks of each other. Next, her one remaining sister died. Then Wilma's husband received the diagnosis of cancer. On the day they learned of his diagnosis, only thirty minutes later they received news of his sister's death from cancer. Wilma witnessed her husband's ups and downs through two major surgeries, through chemotherapy, and then into hospice.

While he was fighting the illness, she realized that she must face her "mind-set that this was the death knell." Turning for understanding to the experiences of God's grace she had encountered, Wilma remembers, "That experience [in her childhood, when she asked her father why God would allow her mother to die and their house to burn] had a major impact on our shared faith and understanding of how God works." Her father had taught her that bad things do happen to God's people, but God promises to be with us always, especially during crisis. Wilma and her husband had to reclaim this truth.

They experienced God's grace as "strength—the strength to deal with what we have to deal [with]." Wilma and her husband found that strength through sharing their thoughts, through prayer, and through the love of others. "His whole response to faith grew. He claimed God's strength. He felt so much love. I think that was the answer. It was God's healing or an awareness of grace or the grace of mystery, still with lots of questions, but a confirmation that God was 'hanging with' him and me."

## REFLECTION

*How have you experienced God's nearness? What happened? What made you aware of the presence of grace during this time?*

Describing God's love, Wilma witnesses, "God is still at work. We don't know what that direction is, and we don't know what the future holds. But the potential of God's love is there, and we should be open to it. I think we need to be receptive to all the possibilities and not have a closed mind against them."

The offer of God's grace is primary. Yes, we pray; we care; we seek to live faithfully; we reach out to others; we serve; and we seek to fulfill our vocations; but grace is the beginning. God's grace offers love, acceptance, and strength. Wilma says, "I'm trying to think of myself in terms more of *who I am* instead of *what I do*. I hope I would be recognized as a caring, listening, compassionate person—someone with an enthusiasm for life, who's open to new experiences and to new ways of sensing God's call and direction in my life." The phrase "who I am" focuses on the grace and gift of life. It is quite powerful to hear these words from a person whose colleagues and friends would describe her as a caring, competent presence, always willing to help others.

After the tragic events of September 11, 2001, many people turned to God. In their fear, uncertainty, and stunned loss, many questioned the values that had driven their lives and turned instead to God's grace and stories of human love and care. Over and over we needed to tell about the firefighters and others who gave up their own lives in an attempt to help people trapped in burning buildings. Over and over we looked for meaning in the rubble, putting up flags and telling one another that getting "back to normal" was a way of displaying our belief in freedom and the values of American culture. These actions soothed us. We also sought ways to help, waiting in long lines to give our blood and our money. We struggled to find a way to respond meaningfully to the chaos and uncertainty.

One way people responded to September 11 was to come to

church. Record numbers filled pews and arrived for memorial services in city plazas and sanctuaries. However, the resurgence of church attendance did not last very long. Three months later, attendance in U.S. Christian churches had returned to normal levels. Too many churches had been unprepared to respond to people's radical shift in priorities or the new urgency to their theological questions.

A research study conducted at that time, December 2001, indicated that people believed their lives had been changed. Many indicated they were trying to focus more on family, and 73 percent expressed a desire to find ways to help others through their jobs. While church attendance has not been maintained, the surge in religious searching continued as people expressed a need to understand other religions and their own faith commitments.[1] Without a doubt, congregations had and still have an important opportunity to assist people in understanding the feelings and faith questions caused by unexpected tragedy.

## Being the Church

Staying focused on God's gracious gift of life keeps our accomplishments and projects in perspective. In our work, we have projects. Often we even think of our recreation and child-rearing as projects. While projects may result in important accomplishments, we risk their becoming the definition of our identity or value. A focus on projects centers life around success and failure. In contrast, a focus on grace reminds us that life itself is a gift. Because we are valuable in God's eyes, we seek to live in response to the gift. When we share love, relationships, and support and build caring communities, we respond to this gift.

Many people searched for community in the weeks and months after September 11. Most people's immediate response to the tragedy was to contact their family. Once we reassured ourselves that our loved ones were alive, we looked around for another way to connect. We participated in prayer services, memorial services, and other symbolic responses. We started displaying the U.S. flag and wearing it on articles of clothing. We sang "God Bless America" at sporting events and felt tears stinging our eyes. We felt connected. Some found vicarious connections in the big telethons that raised money for victims' families. Others involved themselves in fundraising, wanting to buy a new fire truck or something tangible to connect them to those who were at ground zero. And, in record numbers, people went to houses of worship, yearning for an experience of grace. They needed to know God's presence. For a time they were acutely aware that life is a fragile gift.

How can our churches help us focus on life as a gift? As church leaders, how can we view our vocation as an opportunity to share the grace we have received with others? Grace is embodied only as congregations help people face the realities of living, for example, those realities caused by the events of September 11 and the subsequent international military response—realities of brokenness and of hope. Those we interviewed pleaded for truth telling from the church. Obviously, responses to crisis and disruption vary. Denial is one response. It ignores emotions roused by tragedy and attempts to return to life as usual. Another response is insulation, a defense that raises the walls of the fortresses in which we reside.

Grace, in contrast, faces pain and brokenness. Grace enables us to look directly at brokenness with the knowledge that life can be more, that God wants more. Many people in the world live regularly in conditions of terror and anxiety. God created these persons and cares about them just as God cares about us.

Denial and insulation are not faith-filled responses. Rather, grace evidences itself as we accept the commonalities of our humanity, our brokenness and division, and our interconnection. We need to seek to understand the divisions among us, to understand differing religious perspectives and commitments, and to build connections among persons by accepting our common humanity and destiny in the shared world God graciously gave us.

Julia, Lan, and Wilma point to their churches as sources of their knowledge and strength. Each of them responds to God's grace by participating in the ministry of the church. Julia coleads a class on ethics for her church—"ethics in the workplace, ethics in school, ethics as we encounter them with young people, and the larger questions of virtue versus values." Describing one session, she says, "We talked about serious problems on our jobs, where personal conflicts and ethical concerns demanded us to speak up." Moreover, she describes the tone of the group: "We have 'idea safety.' I know there's something happening here. We get a group, not always the same people each week, coming in and saying that this [environment] is safe. I can speak [my opinions and reveal my struggles]."

This group is a public expression of a more intimate group to which she also belongs. "It was the closest thing to a real confessional that I've ever experienced. Each person was going into an area where all it would've taken would have been for somebody to laugh or to say 'How could you?' And yet that wasn't said." The group made available the opportunity for honesty before one another and God, coupled with support for one another and from God. Julia admits, "Whether this particular group will go on forever and ever, I would not be prepared to say. But for everyone, it has been a positive experience, a place of finding acceptance and of continuing Bible study. You come from a Christian basis, and you move out and tie it into your life." As she describes the church, she emphasizes the sharing, trust, and openness "that builds links that last."

## REFLECTION

*What group(s) have you belonged to that built "links that last"? How did the group interact? What aspect of the group's process allowed participants to experience God's support?*

Wilma and Lan, as well as others we interviewed, mentioned the same qualities in groups they appreciate. They used the word *safety* over and over. For them, this word describes how the church points to God's grace. Since September 11, 2001, safety has taken on new meaning. Many U.S. citizens are fearful. They recognize that life is fragile and that destruction can come when we least expect it. Yet many still long for the sense that it is safe to share one's concerns and one's life, and to be open, as Wilma says, "to the God who is still at work in the world. The potential of God's love is there, and we should be open to it." Another said it in the following words: The church can be "the most loving way to be"—a place of respect and service. Penny, a young adult, says, "The church Bible study has let me go into a safe place and argue. Not argue, but struggle and just really understand it." Her congregation allowed her to do the theological reflection she yearned for. "I came out with the knowledge and power of God's Word right there, filling me up."

Two convictions about the church arise from these expressions. First, **the church must invite and welcome our lives, our whole beings.** Recognizing that each of us has been hurt and has fallen short, the faithful church invites these experiences and allows us to tell the truth. Those we interviewed regretted that every church excludes some questions and concerns from conversation. We heard about persons afraid to speak in church about losing a job, about a child who used drugs and alcohol, about an experience of abuse, about a failure, and even about illness when it was a mental illness or a communicable disease like AIDS. At the same time, they made clear that this silencing of concerns limits the church's effectiveness in pointing to grace, forgiveness, and new life. They emphasized that all the concerns of life, even those they could not name in church, require God's guidance.

Eleanor told how she responded to the events of September 11 differently than many of her friends and acquaintances. She felt a calm that came from her faith. "I don't have fear; God will take care of me. I can and do trust in that." In her Sunday school class she raised the theological question of whether Osama bin Laden is a child of God. Her classmates responded with shock. "They think I am either a heretic or a nut to even ask that question!" Eleanor raised an appropriate theological question. Regretfully, the Sunday school class was not a safe place for Eleanor to raise the question. Eleanor pleads, "Will we ever get to the lion and the lamb lying with each other?"

Second, *congregations that most effectively help people explore God's grace exhibit an openness to questions of faith and a seriousness about appropriate theological reflection.* Faith questions and the reflection they prompt should occur in the midst of an intimate, caring community. In fact, Julia spoke of the importance of the church's teaching of its stories, beliefs, rituals, and practices as building blocks for faith. Congregations need to provide contexts for the important work of acquiring the content of our faith *and* practicing theological reflection.

She pointed to her artistic efforts to understand the process of theological reflection. "You know, when you're an artist, you must spend a lot of time in the beginning learning the basics so that you can almost forget them and just go and create—and show that you know the basics without looking stiff." Turning to the subject of theological reflection and ministry, she says: "It [the basics of the faith] has to be in your core, so that no matter whom you meet or respond to, the part of it that is rich comes out. And I don't know how to do that except to immerse yourself in it. And to look for every opportunity."

Theological reflection is not the imposition of a past tradition on experience, nor is it the wooden application of a principle to a particular situation. God is a gracious, living reality whom we meet in old and new ways. God's reality calls us to live in new ways as well as to continue older traditions. Therefore, one cannot search or find the "part that is rich" without efforts to immerse oneself in the story, tradition, and practices. Moreover, this search must occur in a safe community of truth telling—a community of dialogue where one can share insights, listen to others, and seek to respond to God's grace.

For Julia, Lan, and Wilma, small, intentional covenant groups within the church best embody these characteristics. Each one participates in a group for spiritual growth, for discipleship, or for Bible study connected to living. The covenant group provides welcome and safety, as well as intentional efforts to engage in theological reflection in the midst of life's experiences. This reflection honors the church's traditions and practices and seeks for the activity of God, thereby calling participants to new life.

In the weeks after September 11, 2001, our pastor confessed that he felt numb. Nine eleven challenged deeply his pacifist beliefs. As he sought to respond faithfully to the changed world situation, he revisited theological convictions that had seemed settled until then. That confession invited our congregation to revisit their convictions. The honesty and integrity with which our pastor shared his struggle helped create a community of grace and safety where people could open the theological questions relevant to finding faith language for the terrorist attack and the subsequent military response.

**The community of grace must also be a community of acceptance, where truth telling occurs, where persons can share deeply and be respected and heard.** Moreover, the kind of intimacy where individuals can draw on the rich resources of the faith and look with others for God's love and call in the situation also is critical. We return to the image of the spiritual described in chapter 1—that of the welcome table. With expectation and hope growing out of past experiences and glimpses of God's future sumptuous banquet of community and care, we are freed to "shout [our] troubles over" as we "walk and talk with Jesus." The grace-filled church is a welcome table.

# 4

## YEARNING FOR MEANING AND HEALING

Frederick's wisdom was apparent. As he sought to understand the loss and suffering of his beloved wife, Joy, he shared the theological meanings that inspired his actions even in this difficult and hopeless situation. He carried on faithfully, seeking to sustain care for her and hoping that their grandchildren were learning care and compassion. Frederick deeply connects to the gift of grace and God's acceptance at the heart of life itself. He yearned to find meaning and healing in this personal crisis.

Life crises, whether for ourselves or for those we love, bring about deep and passionate yearnings. As human beings we long to make sense of the crises that beset us; the longing is especially urgent when we are hurting. Julia, whom we met in the last chapter, found crisis and loss on every side when her mother died, a best friend died, and her daughter ran away from home. Even in the face of all this hurt, she remained optimistic that God could assuage her pain.

*When have you cried out to God for the oil of healing? What gave you hope in the midst of such stress? In whom could you confide? What question prevailed?*

## Seeking Understanding

Personal crisis often becomes a powerful catalyst for spiritual growth. We all come up against loss or failure or struggles that push us to ask theological questions. Perhaps the most common is, "Why did this happen to me?"

Claude asked that question urgently several times in his life. In his mid-forties when we interviewed him, Claude struggled with his call to ministry with youth. His church did not affirm the call, and he tried to figure out what he should do.

Claude's life story included losses and struggles. For Claude, the very fact that he lived was a miracle. God healed him at the brink of death. He asked himself, "Why did God heal me? What purpose does God have for me?" Even when healing does not occur, especially as miraculously as it did for Claude, we ask why: Why did this suffering and loss happen to my loved one? What can God intend? Where is God's healing balm? What does this mean? We saw these cries also in Eleanor's plea to discover what God intended for her life. Loss and pain dragged her down. This crisis raised profound "why" questions.

Claude was born to middle-aged parents who distanced themselves from him. He spoke of not being allowed in their bedroom except when they punished him. "They did all their stuff in their room, and the room was off-limits. You didn't really want to go up there because if you did, it was bad news."

Claude's father insisted that he attend church and Sunday school. "I went to Sunday school when I was little, screaming all the way," he remembers. But his parents never talked about faith. "It [their faith] was perfectly private. We kids never saw it." Saying grace before meals was the only public expression of faith Claude saw in his parents. "Dad prayed before each meal, same prayer, same voice, every time, morning, noon, and night." The gender roles were clearly divided also. "My dad believed that my mother was the head of the house; she ran the house and he did the business. If she couldn't discipline us kids, she was to let him know, and he would take care of it."

Little Claude found love with his grandmother. "She was the one who was always there in the afternoons when I got home from school. She was the one who hugged me." He remembers her sitting at the piano, joyfully singing "How Great Thou Art" or other hymns. "I would go in her room, get in her bed, and she told me stories about Jesus. She was the kind of person who got up every morning, got dressed, and wanted to help somebody." Claude learned about repentance and God's forgiveness from her.

> When I was little and I would do something wrong and I knew that it was wrong, I would go to my grandmother and say, "What do I do now?" She would say, "Well, let's just talk about it," and then when we got through talking, she would say, "Let's pray," and we would pray about it, and then I would feel okay. What I had done wasn't okay, but I felt better inside.

Claude's parents didn't give him the unconditional love he longed for, but both his grandmother and God provided it.

As a youth, Claude found the love he craved at church. "I felt that I could always go to my church and somebody would be there to love me and to help me to grow, to nurture me." However, he needed more than love—he needed understanding and apparently had to find it on his own.

I lost my best friend in high school, so I know what it is to lose your best friends. I know what it's like on Saturday morning when your mom comes in and says, "Jim was killed last night in an automobile wreck." Or when you call home [from college] and say, "I need to come home. My roommate was killed in an automobile wreck. I just need to come home for the weekend. Can I please come home?" When I called my parents to see if I could come home, I bet somebody a dollar that they would say no. However, they sent me the money for bus fare. They just kinda let me come home. I was hurting. My best friend and now my roommate [had died]. I dreaded going back on Sunday to spend the night in the room by myself. I was a sophomore. I was twenty years old.

The deaths of two close friends within such a short time frame meant a lot of losses for a young man to handle. Claude's retelling of the story provides powerful clues to his need for someone to comfort him and to help him make sense of the fatal accidents. He remembers that he kept asking, "Why me? Why, why me? Why can't my dad hug me? Why can't my mom hug me? Why did my grandmother have to be the one to hug me? Why don't my parents love me? Why can't I do anything right?"

## REFLECTION

*What was your first experience of loss? Who was present with you in the crisis, and how did that person help you make sense of the loss? How did you understand God's activity in that situation?*

Claude finished college, became a corporate accountant, and re-mained with the firm for twenty-three years. He also belonged to one congregation for over twenty years. "My dad taught me that if you make [a commitment], you stick with it even if it gets rough." Yet Claude describes much of his life as "just going through the motions."

Everything came crashing in on him in his thirties. He recalls: "My grandmother died, and then not too long after that I had kidney stones. When I got home from the hospital, my wife informed me that she was divorcing me. Three days later my dad died. I had nowhere to go, so a friend of mine took me in."

A few months after that, Claude contracted pneumonia and then acute hepatitis. His liver shut down. A doctor came into Claude's hospital room to break the news that he would not recover. Soon afterward, a minister came to visit him. This loving soul told Claude confidently, "You will get well. We're going to pray about it right now because I believe in prayer."

They prayed together, and, as Claude reports, "I don't know how to explain it, but I know that there was somebody or something in that room, and during that prayer time my body just felt totally different." Four days later his liver began functioning again, and he started to heal.

## REFLECTION

*Have you experienced a miracle of healing, or do you know someone who has been healed? How do you understand God's activity in this situation?*

In spite of this miracle, Claude's life continued to spiral downward. He couldn't understand or accept the gift of new life given to him. He felt lost and confused about his future and about God's purposes for him. Now Claude believes that he was running away from God. The only person he could talk to about his feelings was a pastoral counselor. Claude recalls, "There was a No Visitors sign on the door of my hospital room so I could say who could come in and who couldn't. I was angry and sick." Deeply depressed, Claude was angry at God and at most of his family and friends.

## REFLECTION

*Think of a time when you felt really angry at God. With whom could you discuss your feelings? What did you learn about God from this experience?*

As he regained his health, Claude struggled to build a new life for himself but made poor choices. He confesses, "I could see myself getting into deep trouble, even though I was still coming to church. But I really felt that the church was not there for me." Like many people facing troubles, Claude "kept asking why." Fortunately he began finding new friends through the church-related preschool his daughter attended. He says, "If it weren't for those people, I probably wouldn't be here right now."

## REFLECTION

Have you gone through periods in your life when you attended church but did not gain anything from going? What or who made the church important again?

# What Does God Want from Me?

Now middle-aged and an active church member, Claude said he'd like to have this epitaph someday: "He tried to be a Christian example for others."

> If someone were introducing me, I'd want him [her] to say that I am a great listener. I love people, especially youth. In the last five years I have really focused on God and the church and realize their importance. I love God first. I love my daughter very much. I try my best to take care of my mother, even though doing so is very difficult.

When we asked what the youth might say about him, he laughed and replied, "He is the most organized human being I've ever known. He needs to loosen up!"

## REFLECTION

*How would you like for someone to introduce you? What five charac-teristics or accomplishments would you identify as the most important of your life? What might someone say about your yearning for God?*

If Claude were to title the current chapter of his life, the title would be "What Does God Want Me to Be?" This title builds on his past miracle and reflects a conflict between Claude and the youth minister. Recently Claude was asked to leave his volunteer position as adult leader for the confirmation class and youth fellowship. This request sparked a huge crisis of vocation for him. Claude's joy in youth ministry is evident. In contrast to the way he feels en route to work, when he drives to church, he says, "I come alive. I'm excited." The prospect of losing his opportunity to work with youth distresses Claude. He reflects:

> God and I have to have a lot more talks than we used to. God doesn't move as fast as I want him to. I wish God would quit testing me. Basically I'm still out there searching in some ways for my calling or where I'm supposed to be. Every time I think I'm where I'm supposed to be, I get a roadblock and have to go a different route. But that's where I am today.

The roadblock of the moment is a request from the youth minister and pastor for Claude to leave youth ministry and find an-other volunteer position in the church. When we interviewed Claude, his demeanor reflected the stress of this difficult situation.

## REFLECTION

*When have you reached a dead end or had a door closed in your face? What truths could you affirm as you faced that crisis? What started you on a road toward healing?*

In spite of this crisis, by the end of our interview Claude could straighten up and declare, "By telling my story, I learned that I'm stronger than I thought I was, and I'm a better survivor than I thought." In addition, he could affirm his earlier miraculous experience of healing and attribute it to God. "There was somebody or something in that room [his hospital room], and that something to me is God."

## REFLECTION

*In what ways have you experienced God's presence, protection, or healing? What was it like? Our research indicates that many persons feel that such stories are unwelcome in their congregation. With whom have you shared this experience?*

God's presence in the midst of pain, loss, and illness emerged as a common theme for persons we interviewed. Seventy-eight-year-old Sophia experienced sixteen months of pain and became unable to walk after a freak accident while straightening bedcovers. She says, "I got really angry. Damn it all! Why should this happen to me? A week ago I felt fine. I am so angry I could die." In the midst of the pain she recalls shouting at God, "When am I going to get over this and get on with my life? This is my life, isn't it?"

A church friend was the only one with whom she could voice that anger. She released her pent-up emotions one day when the friend said, "Sophia, you're putting up such a good front, but I know you're in extreme pain." She said, "I think I yelled at him and said, 'Yes, damn it, I am!'" In the healing that eventually came to Sophia, Psalm 137 became an important passage for her because of its model for bringing our pain to God. Sophia also identified with Job. "I knew how Job felt for the first time in my life. He got angry with his so-called friends, and he got mad because he couldn't find God. Oh, that I might find God!"

## REFLECTION

*When have you been really angry with God? When have you been unable to find God? With whom were you able to share your anger?*

Sophia learned from that crisis to "enjoy living even in hard times. Life is precious; it's a gift; and it is very fragile." After so much pain, she could still affirm, "God never promises us that we won't have pain, injury, or trouble. God promised only one thing, that God will walk with us." But during her sixteen months of disability, Sophia was not always so optimistic.

## REFLECTION

*How have you been able to see God's hand in misfortune or healing?*

Wilma, whose story we told in the last chapter, experienced many losses in her life. Even as a young child she had struggled to make sense of the crisis of losing two homes to fires and the death of her mother. She sought help from her father, a pastor. Then, in middle adulthood, Wilma lost several family members to cancer. Reflecting on these crises, Wilma affirmed the power of community, particularly of a praying community. In each case she "felt surrounded by prayer." She remembered that in the time of both her sister's and her brother's deaths, the community support extended to the ill person and his or her loved ones. "I have experienced God's love through the lived Word," she said with a smile. We yearn for meaning in personal crisis. Wilma found meaning in the love of a Christian community.

Wilma's ultimate experience of Christian community came during the last two and a half months of her husband's life. He chose not to have any more surgery for his cancer and to wait for death at home with hospice care. "We had incredible opportunities to laugh and cry and talk about our joys together. And the church was so much a part of all that. I don't know how people face those things alone without [the support of a faith community]."

## REFLECTION

*When have you felt surrounded by the faith community? What did that experience teach you about God?*

# Seeking Meaning and Healing

When we search for meaning in the midst of crisis, we often go to the church for help. Monty affirmed, "I come [to the church] for answers I don't have." Yet he also admitted that asking for help or even knowing that he might need help was difficult for him.

Monty, a successful engineer and businessman in his late forties, had faced many crises in his lifetime. He served in the Vietnam War. His first marriage ended in divorce, and the child from that marriage struggled with depression and failures. Like many, Monty found that the divorce prompted revisions in his understanding of himself and in his expectations of life. "I think that most significantly I had to come to grips with some key pieces in me. [Old friends helped me] get in touch with a deeper part of me. It [my divorce] kinda jogged me into changing a whole lot of things in my life." The divorce and the challenges of helping his daughter with her problems created a very difficult time in his life. "In retrospect," he muses, "[divorce] was the best thing that ever happened to me. I had to admit that the relationship just wasn't working and that it is okay that my marriage didn't work. I'm going to be okay." The failure of a relationship brings on urgent meaning-making work. Monty was trying to come to terms with the failure and move on with his life. "I guess I'm going through the process of naming the parts of myself that I want to keep and understanding the parts that I need to discard. I'm trying to put together my own place to stand."

## REFLECTION

*When has a failure or another crisis prompted you to look at yourself anew and see that you need to change? How did you make sense of the failure? How did you find a way to understand and accept the failure and your role in it? Where did you recognize God in this process?*

# A Mentor Can Help

Two other themes emerge from the stories of the search for meaning and healing in personal crisis. One theme is the importance of having a mentor who encourages theological reflection. Franz was a boy of fifteen when he was conscripted into the German infantry and forced to become part of the losing effort. "Spring 1945—life was miserable. We ate horse meat, we ate frozen potatoes, rations were horrible, we were cannon fodder. It was hopeless." Although many were corrupted by the miserable situation, Franz, a Lutheran at that time, found support in a good Catholic friend. The two boys began meeting with a Catholic seminarian who was a bit older. "He realized that we had spiritual needs and he would just say, 'Hey, come on over,' and we would talk for a couple of hours." The three of them spent many hours talking. Franz calls it "spiritual nurture at a time of utter drought."

At night the ragtag infantry with their antiaircraft guns often moved to a new location. As he traveled in the darkness with a sense of urgency, Franz noticed crucifixes in churchyards (from Easter services). A few weeks later, Franz was badly wounded. One of the few survivors, he struggled through the woods until a priest sheltered him. Eventually he surrendered to American forces who sent him to a hospital for prisoners of war, where he recovered. He survived that time of terror with "a Bible in my pack, a memory of crucifixes along the way, a Catholic friend, and constant prayer in my heart." The few weeks preceding the wound were "short but intense," and Franz still carries letters from the seminarian with their theological teachings in his Bible. Those intense times of theological reflection had prepared Franz for the trials of being wounded and captured.

## REFLECTION

*During what times in your life have you sought a teacher or mentor who seemed spiritually more mature as you prepared for an impending crisis? How did the images or concepts you learned during the time of preparation shape your response to the crisis?*

Now, more than fifty years later, Franz reflects, "It is wrong to ask why God let something happen. God does not protect us from life's difficulties, but God is in life's difficulties." Note how this conviction communicates a God who shares our pain. In God's loving presence, we find strength to face our difficulties and continue.

## When We're Not Good Enough

Another kind of crisis may occur when we experience good that seems undeserved. Jimmie, who struggled with addictions most of his life, tried to get his life together at age twenty-nine. Sober for a year, he wondered why he had survived. "Too many crazy things have happened to me, too many good things in the last couple of years. Honest to God, when I try to explain all these good things, I don't believe in coincidences anymore." Jimmie found an accepting community in his congregation, yet he admitted to being terrified.

Like Eleanor, who yearned for meaningful work consistent with her faith, Jimmie found that his escape from life-threatening danger stimulated theological questions. He thought perhaps God's hand influenced his escape, but he needed to search for what this event might mean for his life.

Struggle and pain are not the only situations that lead us to yearn for meaning. The crisis of good fortune or an escape from danger also stimulates our yearning for meaning and healing. When has a good situation caused you to wonder about its meaning? What evidence of God's hand might be seen in this situation?

# The Believer and the Church

The issues of personal loss and hurt often serve as major catalysts for a faith quest. The classic question is one of theodicy: How can a loving God allow evil and suffering to exist in personal lives, in our communities, and in our world? Theologians and faithful believers have examined this question. Some seek to answer it by highlighting the completeness of God's vision and the partiality of our own. Persons who adhere to this view hope that ultimately everything will turn out for the best. Frankly, none of the people we interviewed found this explanation satisfactory.

Others see loss and suffering as the result of sin. While we all know that disobedience, alienation, and violence committed against others do bear a cost, there seems to be no justice in the amount of suffering that exists. The most vulnerable and innocent are sometimes victims of hurt and loss. The great expression of hurt reflected in Job 24 provides an example of the depth of loss and pain and a cry for healing for the innocent. Sin does not provide a comprehensive answer to the presence of suffering.

> "They [the wicked] thrust the needy off the road;
>     the poor of the earth all hide themselves.
> Like wild asses in the desert they go out to their toil,
>     scavenging in the wasteland food for their young.

They reap in a field not their own
    and they glean in the vineyard of the wicked.
They lie all night naked, without clothing,
    and have no covering in the cold.
They are wet with the rain of the mountains,
    and cling to the rock for want of shelter.
"There are those who snatch the orphan child from the
breast,
    and take as a pledge the infant of the poor. . . .

. . . . . . . . . . . . . . . . . . . . . . . . . . . . . . . . . . . . . . . .

"From the city the dying groan,
    and the throat of the wounded cries for help;
    yet God pays no attention to their prayer."
                    —Job 24:4-9, 12

Laments of healing and searching for meaning in loss, tragedy, and mistreatment fill the Psalms. The persons we interviewed repeatedly turned to the promise that God "knows the hairs of our heads," that God "clothes the lilies of the fields," and that God stands with us in pain and tragedy.

In other words, the questions of theodicy, of loss and healing, stand central to our theological reflection. All of the answers seem limited, but the questions remain. Some moments of deepest meaning come when a person experiences God in the midst of the pain itself. In those situations the healing God is not experienced as a miracle worker but as a sustaining and loving presence of grace even in the midst of loss and hurt. Part of our vocation, then, is to join with God's gracious presence and to stand with those who suffer.

## REFLECTION

In what ways does your congregation stand with those who suffer? What consequences of faith emerge for those who suffer? What consequences emerge for the faithful?

# 5

## YEARNING FOR JUSTICE

When we wrote this book, in the summer of 2001, several young men, seemingly in the prime of their health and strength, died suddenly on the football field. It was the "Summer of Why?" The headline in the September 2, 2001, edition of the *Chicago Tribune* read, "In this day . . . why are we dying?" The story told about six young men, all football players from twelve to twenty-two years of age, who died from heatstroke, heart conditions, asthma, or other exercise-induced conditions. While reporting the stories of these young men, their teams, and their families, this public newspaper asked the question why?

Seeking to answer the question, the author, Philip Hersh, turned to Thornton Wilder's reflection in *The Bridge of San Luis Rey* about the death of five persons from the collapse of a bridge in Peru. Hersh wrote:

> "Why did this happen to those five?" Wilder has one of his characters ask. "If there were any plan in the universe at all, if there were any pattern in a human life, surely it could be discovered latent in those lives so mysteriously

cut off," the author continued. "Either we live by accident and die by accident, or we live by plan and die by plan."[1]

That a public news article would ask these deepest questions of why, of whether we live and die by accident or by plan, is significant. Everyone asks these questions. The deaths of these athletes caused pain and tears for the victims' families and friends. Why wasn't an enlarged heart discovered before a child died on an athletic field? Why does a young man give all he has and more, even when his temperature rises to dangerous levels? Why do young men experiment with and risk the effects of strength-inducing drugs? Why are sports and games so important that we risk the lives of our youth for an advantage in a "game"?

Moreover, the summer also ended with people asking why two young men, one in Des Moines and the other in Oakland, each killed members of his own family, including children. Or why calls for peace from both Israelis and Palestinians continued to go unheeded while people on both sides divided into factions, killed one another and innocent victims, and destroyed homes. In these last two instances, we can see mental illness, rage, and long-standing grievances as factors. The evil seems more understandable because of the evil or brokenness of the perpetrators. Still we ask: Why does a child die on a practice field when he or she seems healthy and is surrounded by advanced medical facilities? Or why do workmates refuse to trust one another and seek to undercut the goals of the workplace? Why do some families break apart when loss confronts them? Why are our best intentions sometimes not enough?

Then the calendar turned to September 11, 2001. A beautiful, blue-sky day was interrupted by planes flying into the Twin Towers of the World Trade Center in New York; a plane smashing into the Pentagon in Washington, D.C.; and another crashing in the Pennsylvania countryside. These events—acts of terrorists—and the subsequent military and security responses heightened the earlier why questions. All of North America and many other countries of the world went on high alert, uncertain what might happen next. People went to the deepest parts of themselves to ask why and to seek the calming presence of God. Memorials, prayer services, and other communal expressions of mourning became highest priority. Some congregations sought to protect neighbors who were abused because of their religion or ethnicity. The months that followed brought recession, war, and fear. In the midst of the loss and uncertainty, many spoke of the need for "justice, not revenge" as they struggled to know how to respond.

These questions of why remain, at their heart, questions about loss, illness, brokenness, and theodicy. We ask: Why do we individually experience loss and death? Why do injustice and death rain on others? Claude commented to us about his passion for youth ministry, "When you see their hurt and you can offer hope, you do not stand aside." Issues of justice and injustice, of evil and healing, raise fundamental religious questions for persons of faith.

## REFLECTION

*What kinds of situations do we face that make us ask why? What kinds of happenings prompt the why questions? What assumptions do we have about God's power and will?*

In the next few pages, we draw on the adolescent and adult experiences of two persons we interviewed to explore these questions of injustice. Both served in World War II, one as a seventeen-year-old soldier for the Allies, the other as a fifteen-year-old antiaircraft gunner for the Germans. Today both are successful community leaders and devout churchmen in congregations in the United States. Both seek to live out the grace they have experienced in their vocations and through the ministries of the church. Perhaps their reflections and their lifelong search for justice can illumine the current world situation.

# The Enemy Is Like Us

Thomas, trained as an engineer and lawyer, served for several years as the vice-president of a major corporation and now commutes between Washington, D.C., and his home in Chicago. In Washington, he works for a major business news magazine. He told us that his religious questions were defined by his adolescent years spent in the infantry in World War II. "I began to grow up then because when I went to Europe, I saw what horror there was."

At sixteen he and some friends enlisted in the army. "As young boys, we wanted the adventure. We thought we weren't doing our part—our responsibility." When their ages were discovered, they were sent home. At seventeen, he enlisted again. He received his father's permission "even though my father had been in World War I. I know how awful it must have been for him to give permission."

After basic training, he moved to "jump school" (training for paratroopers). Then he had that crucial formative experience. As a part of a group of soldiers near Bergen-Belsen, he participated in the liberation of a concentration camp. Meeting the victims has haunted him. "It was a terrible experience and one that was a surprise. We didn't know anything about the camps. I was just eighteen."

The brutality, suffering, and evil he witnessed sent him on a journey to seek understanding. "Seeing these abject, almost dead victims was something I didn't understand." Moreover, despite the number of Christian clerics who spoke out against the Holocaust and lost their lives, he views the silence as well as complicity of many church leaders as "a monumental failure of Christianity." In addition, he regrets that even his own nation attempted to hide the Holocaust. He says that it "was an anti-Semitic, smug, surface-Christian nation."

He described a disconnection between his military training and his experience of real people.

I'd been trained—trained to be a killer, trained to hate. And then all of a sudden, I saw the enemy, and he is not like the poster. He's sick, and has children, and parents, and they're wounded, and they're abject, and some of them are awful, and some of them are very much victims. It was a complicated and confusing thing.

How can one comprehend suffering and the evil that human beings commit against one another? Evil loomed in the forces that instigated and carried out the Holocaust, in the compliance of institutions (including churches) and individuals; it was embodied in those who coldheartedly murdered and tortured others; it victimized German young people; and it was present in the liberating nation that remained smugly anti-Semitic.

Returning to the United States to engineering school, Thomas continued to ask why. He gathered regularly with other GIs to "explore the beginnings of ideas." Because of his own internal collision of values, he served for a time in a reserve training command, always taking the opportunity "to read in Carnegie libraries around the country. God bless Carnegie!"

## REFLECTION

*How has your search for an answer to "why" shaped your life? Have you joined groups in search of answers? read books? sought out experts?*

After ignoring a set of orders, Thomas found himself back serving in the military in Korea. "I was still a GI. I let my reserve [status] lapse and ignored it. I got called back and started all over as a private. It was a horrible mess, a stupid problem, and an awful, dumb period of life. Getting yelled at by corporals all over again— it was just bad." Nevertheless, he had what he calls "mental privacy" that allowed him to read, study, wonder, and question.

During this time Thomas thought about the church a great deal. Most of his experiences with the church had been "really shallow and negative. But my mother's strength seemed somehow related to her being a religious person. She prayed. Even though she wasn't very articulate, she simply had a feeling that connected her with religious belief." What a contrast between her and Thomas's experiences. He wanted both intellectual searching and emotional security.

To him the intellectual shallowness of religious institutions was obvious: "The ministers were nice guys, but they were not addressing serious questions. They were burying serious questions or denying their existence." And, in contrast, the depth of his mother's faith kept offering an emotional connection that continued to encourage him to search.

> I found myself continually struggling with the questions of religion. I think because they're basic human questions: we're all born, we all die, we all suffer, and we all know suffering. I'd seen death early. I'd seen horrible things. I couldn't put it all together.

Through night law school, indigent prisoner defense work, exhaustion with litigation, and then a stint in corporate leadership, Thomas's career continued to develop. He sought out one church after another, looking for intellectual stimulation and emotional security, but he found neither. He worked as a Scout leader and invested himself in public service. He moved through a series of church communities seeking a home for his children, yet they were never enough. Nonetheless, his religious curiosity never died. Neither did his fear that "some of the worst evils in the world are wrought in the name of religion."

## REFLECTION

*What situations does the church address or fail to address today that you would identify as complying with or participating in evil? What are you doing about this evil?*

Thomas has finally found a congregation that brings together community, intellectual curiosity, honesty, and worship. He defines community in the following way: "Part of the process of being a religious person is communal. You have children, you have common interests, and you live near one another. There are a lot of common points." He describes his particular congregation as "full of love that allows for little groups of us who are more kindred than the others. Yet I don't feel a lack of kindred spirit with others in the church with whom I know I would disagree. There is a civility that's engendered here in a sacred place."

Thomas's story of the church's accepting him, even with all his questions and his insatiable searching nature, expresses intellectual curiosity and honesty, or theological reflection. "Then, for the first time in my life, I heard from the pulpit a minister translating scripture into my real world and lacing it with wonderful humor. He invited me into conversation, and it continues."

Thomas speaks of the connection between worship and emotion: "It [finding a church home] was such an experience. I get choked up just thinking about it. Like all people, I hungered for a place to worship, and I found it." He continues: "Religion is so pervasive; it is not something that is imposed. It comes out of us. We are religious primates."

The languages of science, law, and litigation he had learned now combined with the language of religion. In this community of faith, Thomas found a bridge. He belongs to a group of professional persons—doctors, researchers, lawyers, and business leaders—that meets each month to read a book and discuss faith and vocation. Thomas views religious language as profoundly powerful; it is a language of participation and of poetry that focuses our living with the deepest of human emotions and questions. "Religion, poetry, a participant, stories, metaphors, emotional certainty, belief, and faith—all that stuff goes together."

The bridge remains important for him. He confesses:

Now it's possible for me to read and hear biblical stories, including the historical and critical approach. That's just marvelous freedom. You can reach within and embrace the biblical tradition as a story and recognize the importance of emotional certainty, which is really what belief is about. When people demand scientific or legalistic certainty from a metaphor, they are in trouble. And when people deny the truth of a metaphor, emotional truth, they are in trouble. So now I have a way of dealing with and crossing these bridges of language, back and forth.

*Participation* is the word Thomas uses to describe the language of his faith. To him, participation is a call—a call to be part of the community that is the church, a call to share in the mystery and emotional connections that are part of the "sacred mystery" of the faith, a call to search with intellectual honesty the traditions of the faith and their power to help us understand and act in the present, and finally a call to justice.

With justice, we return to the questions that his experience as an eighteen-year-old in the Holocaust called forth. "Justice is [constructed by humans] or it's not made. Justice is up to us." The commitment to justice and the reality of the presence of evil, even in our own traditions, "increases our obligations to one another." We are called to live the faith. Thomas views persons in justice seeking and justice service as models of the Christian life.

## REFLECTION

*How do you respond to Thomas's conviction that justice is up to us? How is justice a theological issue for you?*

Thomas embodies commitment to justice by working in his own community for healing among Jews and Christians. "We have responsibility to be just to one another and to the earth upon which we live and to all things in it." Thomas initiated a community-wide remembrance of *Kristalnacht*, the "Night of Broken Glass" (November 9–10, 1938) when the Germans ransacked Jewish businesses and synagogues, beginning the pogroms and the Holocaust. This remembrance and the conversations and relationships it has inspired provide one example of a life lived in confession and solidarity, a life seeking justice.

## REFLECTION

*How can we embrace confession and solidarity in our worship? What would including these acts mean for our relationship with God? With one another?*

His encounters with brutalized prisoners of the Holocaust, with enemies who were also human, and with a spirit of meanness in the Allies sent Thomas as a young man on a lifelong search for answers to why we suffer and impose suffering on others. And Thomas is not alone, for the yearning for justice is a common cry of the people of God.

# Is Anything Solid during Chaos?

"I needed things to hold me together. The church stayed in the picture." Franz, a year younger than Thomas and a teenage soldier in the army of Germany, stands in contrast to Thomas. A leader in his congregation, Franz now lives in the United States.

At the end of the European sector of World War II, Franz was a badly wounded seventeen-year-old German youth recuperating in a U.S. field hospital. Because his mother lived in New York, he was allowed to apply for transport to the United States. Franz had not seen his mother since his parents' divorce when he was two years old. She had married a Jewish surgeon and immigrated first to Italy and then to the United States. Franz and his mother lost contact after the U.S.

entry into the war in 1941. Yet, late in 1945, American occupation personnel, friends of his mother, reestablished contact. Through their efforts and those of the Red Cross, Franz began the thirteen-month project of applying for immigration.

American relief efforts allowed Franz to immigrate. His mother's citizenship, plus the facts that he had refused Nazi party membership and spoke some English (his foster mother, born in the United States, taught him some English ), provided the foundation for the move, which took place in February 1947. Soon after Franz arrived in the United States, his mother and her surgeon husband divorced. This left him with little "financial and ideological support." By grace, a university admitted him, and he majored in business and economics. We told him Thomas's story. As he heard it, he mused:

> Soldiers learn that they're all in a crappy situation, regardless of which side. It gets cold and miserable. Perhaps the American soldier has better cigarettes and better rations, but it's a mess either way. We had no feelings of personal animosity. We realized they were doing their thing and we were doing ours. We beat one another up and wondered, Who's winning this thing, anyway?

Franz had a confusing childhood. After his parents' divorce when he was two, he spent two years in a children's home until an aunt in Heidelberg took him as a foster child. From 1939 to 1941, he attended a "tough, hard, highly disciplined boys' school that filed me down and sandpapered me." The school was a paramilitary setup, heavily into proclaiming National Socialism. "There were flags everywhere; we had three inspections every day; there was lots of discipline; and the atmosphere was very patriotic." The purpose of the school was to produce "corporate children."

At fifteen Franz was drafted into an antiaircraft division of the army. He says, "We were one-third school boys, one-third Hitler youth (compulsory), and one-third soldiers." While the drafting had been couched as a national need and a form of school, with teachers sent into the batteries, Franz says, "We were 98 percent soldiers."

Describing the days as a soldier, he says, "It [being a soldier] was a common occurrence. Not so easy, but we all were in it. We made the best of it and prayed for the war to come to an end. We could never think very far because you think about survival, about rations, about the endless duties—cleaning weapons, ammunition, and stuff like that."

Raised in the German Evangelical tradition, Franz learned early that church was "held in serious and high respect." From the religious education in the school of his early childhood years, he respected a teacher, Professor Kaiser, who with "kindness and authority" provided a foundation in a chaotic world. During the chaos of the war years, his drafting, service, wounding, and waiting, he confides: "A chaos was underway. And yet I knew there was something solid." That something was the message of the Christian faith. He thought, "It [Christianity] has been around for 1900 years. The message was a supportive one; it was uplifting. And I needed that." He describes those days: "I suffered under others who were tyrants. I learned how to assert myself. You had to be weak in your head not to realize that Germany could lose the war. Then came the clarity that the whole Nazi ideology was a heathen thing."

Looking back at confirmation class in which he participated from 1941 to 1943 in a local Lutheran church, Franz reflects on a faith that profoundly shaped him for the events that were to come. He describes his confirmation experience.

> We went twice a week into a minister's study, learning about everything from hymns to church history. [The minister was] a wonderful man, decisive, warmhearted, and passionate. The times made him harder and harsher. He really thundered against the happenings of the times from a spiritual point of view. I learned later that he was a

minister in the Confessing Church [those who opposed the war and the Nazi ideology]. This man had immense influence. I have his confirmation certificate—a picture of Jesus and my signature, hanging in my room. He definitely equipped me. I toted my Bible with me everywhere.

Franz experienced the incarnation of faith after becoming wounded. "Then came the 10th of April, 1945, eleven o'clock in the morning. Five tanks came over the hill and shot the daylights out of us. Just about the only survivor and badly wounded, I hid in the woods. A Catholic priest took me in after others said no." Risking his own safety, the priest saved Franz's life.

Franz's biblical faith was crucial for him as he immigrated, again experienced a family breakup, and entered the university. His career developed, sometimes up and sometimes down. It necessitated moving often. He attended church, he now says, for the wrong motives. "I wanted something out of it; I wanted the assurance of healing, fixing up problems." Looking back over his early losses and those who cared for him, he discovered a need to hold onto something.

Reflecting on the war, he realized he had to deal with the shame of "what Germany had done and what he felt about it." He saw that "war is horrible" as well as the efforts of soldiers to smash one another. The German "political guilt problem" is an important question for him.

What was difficult in a way was to come [to the United States] and [to face] my mother's second husband, a Jewish surgeon who had lost three people in the camps— his former wife, his mother, and his brother. There was not a meal in those first months where we did not discuss the Holocaust. I had thought with time this would pale out, but it really hasn't. As time has gone on, the horrors have become more unexplainable, more inexcusable. They have become a stone wall where my feeling and reasoning abilities are at a standstill.

No longer concerned about receiving what he needs, Franz now speaks about the church in new ways: "The Lord has tapped me on the shoulder. I have had no Damascus road experience, but things have become clearer." Active in his church and in a men's group filled "with spirit, mutual respect, communal prayer, and work for soup kitchens, missions, and community counseling," Franz now teaches/leads two small covenant Bible study and service groups.

## REFLECTION

*How do you view the church? In what ways does it meet your needs? What role of the church emerges as most important for you?*

Franz's congregation attends to the wholeness of its people—to their emotions, spirits, minds, and bodies. There people find "uplifting, self-esteem, and priorities." Through his teaching and service he seeks to encourage others and to help them discover the best priorities. Clearly a wonderful listener and thoughtful learner, he invites others to share their lives and to examine moments of life in light of the traditions and practices of Christianity.

Franz argues, almost like the Confessing Lutheran pastor of his childhood, "What life would we have without the church? Where are the restraining influences in our society for social well-being and justice? They come from the churches!" He proclaims that he is "pleased to witness what God has done in his life." He works with others through study and prayer to help them to see the grace of God, to understand living in relationship to God, and to engage them in working for social well-being and justice.

Franz affirms, "I have three families: my own family, my work family, and my church family. Privately I add a fourth, my divine family, the Trinity." He sees the humanity and divinity of Jesus as keys to faith. Franz believes that Jesus' invitation, "Follow me," "is the most important, the most beautiful, and the most challenging [invitation of all]." He thinks that one deals with evil and suffering in the world by confronting it, by "struggling with the questions," by asking, together in a covenantal community, questions of "the Bible and seeing what answers come."

Franz believes that raising the question "Why did God let the Holocaust happen?" is not enough. The answers are obvious: "Because thousands and thousands of people planned it with purposeful, heinous energy" and "Because others complied." The fuller question is, "Where was God?" (or "Where is God in this situation?") Franz now answers this question by saying, "God lived in those who helped others in the camps. God stands with people in need."

Franz confesses, "I let myself go into swamps with doubt and fear. How could I not admit it?" Then, with a wry smile, he says, "Don't take this wrong, but the part of Jesus I see in my inner perspective is his backside. Why? Because he walks ahead of me, turning now and then, to see if I'm coming. I seldom see him face-to-face because he always looks with concern at others." The direction of Jesus' gaze provides a model for Franz's gaze. Having experienced new life, Franz openly and honestly works with others seeking new life.

## A Public, Accountable Practice

In speaking about the importance and validity of Christianity, Thomas calls it "a communal, public, accountable practice." He further adds, "This makes the difference between Christianity and fiction." There are no easy answers for broken relationships, for evil in the world, and for suffering. Both Thomas and Franz have experienced suffering and hurt, as we all do to varying degrees. Both feel that faithful living can best be found in the struggle with others to understand, to see God in the midst, and to work for new life in real, particular situations.

Franz clarifies his understanding of vocation: "I'm in financial services work. That work doesn't have anything to do with God's kingdom in any verbal or any direct way. After a long, long while, it finally dawned on me that what the Lord wants us to do is to do that work, in those outside places—financial services for me—in such a manner that we rely on faith teachings to best see how it should be done." He has begun to experience "all of life as ministry."

## REFLECTION

*Our baptism calls us to serve God and others. How does that calling connect to the idea that all of life is ministry? Identify portions of your life you do not consider ministry. Why do you view them this way?*

Here we return to the interrelationship of the yearnings of the people of God. We embody the yearning for vocation as we attend to the faith in our everyday actions. These actions are grounded in the awareness of God's acceptance and grace and in recognition of human loss, illness, injustice, and brokenness. We graciously respond to God's love through service and, moreover, because of God's grace, we seek to alleviate the hurt we see. That is how life is to be lived!

Yet Christian faith involves a particular way of being, or, as Thomas says, "a public, accountable practice." We struggle to accept grace; we respond to need; and we discover vocation only through attending to the practices of the faith within community. Assisting with this struggle are the "practices," or what John Wesley called the *means of grace*. Giving attention to worship and prayer focuses us on the presence and spirit of God in the world. Participating in the sacrament of baptism and sharing in the baptisms of others remind us that life is God's gift. Participating in the sacrament of Holy Communion, we remember the life and ministry of Jesus and, moreover, we encounter the promise and reality of God's new life that is present even in the midst of great evil and death. Joining with others in studying the scriptures, praying, and making commitments, we find support for being faithful to our unique and particular calls for ministry in everyday life. These public, accountable practices guide us in faithfulness.

September 11, 2001, brought sudden death and destruction to the shores of the United States. As persons of faith reflected on the evil acts of that day, they yearned to understand why and to know how to respond justly. Although evil actions need accountability, returning evil for evil is not an adequate answer to the question of how to respond justly. Defining justice may elude us.

Part of the answer remains to be discerned. This discernment involves the difficult work of revealing brokenness at the heart of the American lifestyle, struggling to understand how to live with difference, and responding appropriately to persons who want to destroy a way of life and the people who live it. As we struggle with these questions, we will need courage. That can be drawn from the one certainty: God remains faithful. This fact calls us to reflect, to assess, to listen, to understand, and to reach out to others as fellow children of a gracious God.

Even with the gifts of these practices, means of grace, we have heard three other yearnings from God's people. First is the yearning to know that what we together discover is indeed faithful to God; in other words, we yearn for assurance. Second is the yearning for acceptance. Our interviews revealed that we (the people of God) cannot engage in the search for assurance unless our confusions and questions are honored and we are accepted as fellow pilgrims and travelers seeking faithfulness. And, third, the reality of God's grace and the glimpses of community that gives new life call us to face the world, yearning and working for the new creation promised in the vision of the kingdom of God and the welcome table—the banquet of fine foods and fine wines where people from all ends of the earth gather in harmony and community. May it be so!

# 6

## YEARNING FOR ASSURANCE

"Homo sapiens are hurt animals. They need a safe harbor," said Monty. Religious faith is part of the safe harbor Monty was speaking of. Although many people can identify faith questions, and some can live without clear answers or with ambiguous ones, they also recognize that we need to find a center that will hold. Monty called it "a place to stand." Without that place to stand, we do not know how to make decisions about what is right and wrong or what choices we should make. From this center flow the values that shape our lives.

How do we know the truth of the promise of God's love? How do we know that the service we render will make a difference? How do we know our hopes will be fulfilled? In the midst of joy and crisis, how does faith assure us?

Sometimes the center gets a bit shaky. Developmental theorists have observed that people who are unsure of their center feel anxious. They struggle tenaciously to hold on to the center as long as they can, even though it is inadequate. Some marriage therapists speak about how couples too often seek counseling only after enormous pain has built up or the vitality of the relationship has cooled because they have taken the center for granted without being sensitive to the changes that were occurring.

Eventually, however, many of us have to remake our center a bit as we learn more about life and about ourselves. We will work hard to regain a place of equilibrium. Thomas, whose life quest has been to address suffering and evil, recognizes that people do not want their center "to unravel." A lot of people have "this terrible need for emotional certainty," observed Monty. They "cling to that." They want to be assured that their center will hold.

Fanny J. Crosby's 1873 hymn "Blessed Assurance" expresses that need. Its chorus affirms the center with the words, "This is my story, this is my song, praising my Savior all the day long." Human beings find focus and comfort in a faith story that gives meaning to their lives. We long for that blessed assurance that we fit into God's plan and that we know where we stand.

## Trusting the Promises

Some people satisfy their yearning for assurance by choosing to live as a Christian disciple. Often they make this choice as a young adult and do not feel a need to revisit it later in life. This center provides direction for the rest of their life.

Terri, age forty, is one example of a person who made a choice for Christian discipleship and has found it to provide that assurance. Terri paraphrased Philippians 3:10: "My determined purpose is that I may know [Christ]." That determined purpose has guided her since she made a decision in college.

A friend led me through about five weeks of study before she asked, "Can you see any reason why you should not invite Christ into your life?" I answered, "No." This was a very factual decision, to invite Christ into my life.

Once she made the decision, Terri was comfortable with it.

With Christ in her life she feels assured that she is on the right track. This decision provides the certainty and order for which she yearned. Nothing in her life has challenged the center so far.

## REFLECTION

*Have you made a decision for Christian discipleship? Who influenced you in that process? If you have not yet made that decision, what issues remain open for you? What would you need to know to be able to feel certain that you want to be a Christian disciple?*

After Terri determined her purpose, other choices came more easily. Although certified as a teacher, Terri devoted her first several years after college graduation to working with an evangelical organization. For a while, working with this group seemed faithful to her determined purpose. But Terri was also a young American, influenced by cultural values of independence and equality. Eventually she began to question the hierarchical nature of the organization, especially in regard to gender. She said with a smile, "I guess I'm a fundamentalist feminist!" By *fundamentalist*, she meant deeply believing the Christian story; by *feminist*, she meant valuing her own experiences and equality of the genders.

After coming to this realization during mission work in Japan, Terri returned to the United Methodist suburban church she had attended before college. In her zeal for the evangelical organization and its mission, she had criticized her former congregation. "As I thought back through what had occurred, I realized that I had given nothing to this church. I had not let them know me in any way. I had not tried to get to know them. I had just come to take." So she came back to her home church with clear purpose to be involved, to use her gifts and graces in the life of the church, and to be intentional about spiritual growth.

The certainty that her most important value is to know God in Jesus Christ still guides her. Terri believes she cannot fulfill her commitment to God without being part of a church. "Without the rest of the saints, you ain't gonna get there!"

Terri says, "I can find my greatest joy by being a catalyst for other people, and letting other people be a catalyst for me." Her choice has guided many decisions in her life. That determined purpose is certain for Terri even while she seeks the right place to embody it.

## REFLECTION

*How would you describe the role of your church community in your commitment to discipleship? What aspects of congregational life help you most as you search for a certain and orderly center for your life? Sermons? A prayer group? Friends? A class?*

## Revisiting the Choices

Monty, however, has found that he needs to revisit his early decisions. At age fifty, Monty is a successful engineer and businessman. Soft-spoken and well-dressed, he meets others gently and listens carefully. He travels worldwide, installing the brains of cellular telephone systems in countries all around the world. When we interviewed him, he had just finished a project in Southeast Asia where telephone wires had never been laid but where people in isolated villages could connect to the rest of the world through their new cellular telephones. He is an active member of a suburban Protestant congregation in the Midwest and had recently completed training in small-group spiritual leadership.

However, the road to this congregation was marked by several challenges to his assurance. As a high school student, Monty saw what he called "the hypocritical nature of religion and church." He observed people who always attended church doing things he considered unethical. During the Vietnam War, he went to college but did not apply himself. Consequently he was drafted.

The small-town Texas faith Monty grew up with proved inadequate. "When you're near death, dodging bullets, you can get in touch with a lot of things real quickly. One of the toughest things for me to deal with was learning to trust the other guys in my platoon. You depend on those others for life. It is almost a religious experience." He began to sort out his early understandings. "I guess I was going through the process of naming the parts that I wanted to keep, and understanding the parts that I thought were wrong. I came from a small town in Texas where you wave the flag and eat apple pie." Those simple values were insufficient for his experience in that complicated war.

Monty survived the war. He went back to school, married, fathered a child, and became successful professionally. Then the child was diagnosed with an emotional illness, and after a time the marriage disintegrated. Monty's wartime experience had prompted a critical look at the faith of his childhood and left him unable to trust the church. "In that phase I was very, very cynical, and I felt manipulated."

A new marriage and family became the starting point for a new look at the church. "I primarily did it for my wife, because I would not have gone into one by myself. I gave the church another chance, and I really did begin to see some good things for me there." He had spent about fifteen years fully immersed in his career and caring for a child with emotional disabilities. He had not paid much attention to the part of himself that yearned for assurance of God's care. "I guess for the first time I paid a little bit of attention to my own needs."

Paying attention has brought Monty to a new place of assurance. "If you open yourself up and you listen, this thing that is God will give you information if you can hear it. You have to work to listen. You have to work real hard to listen." He agreed to participate in an intensive training for small-group process. Through participation in that group Monty experienced the grace of God. "They listened; they prayed; and they got me to a place where I could listen, or I could hear, or I could appreciate." Now he is coming back to the faith lessons from childhood. "My parents gave me most of the tools," he admits. And now Monty says, "I discounted a lot of my early religious teachings because I didn't think they applied to me. Now I wish I knew more about the Bible because I see it is very rich in things that could help me."

The trauma of war and family disintegrations obliterated the assurance Monty had possessed as a small child—that faith was mostly about going to church and obeying a few rules. He has returned to the values of the religious community and Christian traditions. Nurtured by a small group of other persons who seek assurance of God's guidance, he has learned to listen and has received assurance.

## REFLECTION

*How do you view the faith of your childhood? Have you claimed faith in a fresh way? What started you on that journey? Like the hymn writer, have you come to a place of blessed assurance? What helped you to find assurance of God's presence again?*

## A Faith That Makes Sense

For some of us, the yearning for assurance is satisfied by a faith that makes sense. Faith needs to have some internal logic. We look for congruence with our own experiences or with the world as we see it. Bill has found certainty in his faith because it makes sense to him and is congruent with his observation of the creation. Bill is a forty-six-year-old mechanical engineer with a wife and children. He is slim and energetic, his handshake firm.

Bill grew up as a Baptist. His life has been orderly and successful; he has never faced a major failure or loss. Early in their marriage Bill and his wife belonged to a small congregation that was, according to Bill, "in the early stages of catching on fire." Bill describes their membership in that congregation as an "awakening."

In that setting he learned the joy of Christian discipleship and community. Bill described it:

> Then we started to get to know these people and started to see what their lives were like. It was like all of a sudden, by their living example, our eyes became open and we said, "Now I understand what these verses are about." And we started saying, "Hey! This makes sense!"

Bill compared the messages he had heard throughout his life from the Bible and the church to the way of life he observed in this congregation, and this confirmed for Bill the truths of the Christian tradition. It fit together and made sense to him. Bill and his wife found close friends in their Sunday school class, which consisted mostly of young couples. They became like family. "Whenever somebody was in trouble or had a good time, we got together and celebrated," Bill says.

## REFLECTION

*What experiences of community have assured you of the truths of Christian faith? When have you experienced a community that became like a family? How did you find that group? What kind of commitments did it require of you? What effect did being a part of that community have on your life?*

Not only was Bill's class a social outlet, but class members were learning the meaning of being Christian disciples.

> You began to see how people lived the Christian life, an openly Christian life. And what a difference it made on not only what they did on Sunday morning, but also what they did on Tuesday and Wednesday and Thursday and

Friday. And you said, "Hey, this makes sense. I can do that."
You had a whole group that was basically trying to support one another, trying to walk the talk.

## REFLECTION

*Who has exemplified the Christian life for you? Who has influenced
you most in living more faithfully? How do these examples help you
know that faith makes sense?*

For twelve years, Bill and his wife were part of that congregation. Then they moved to new jobs in another state. Trying to find
a new church home that felt as good as the last one proved difficult. Bill and his wife finally chose a church near their home and
have struggled to make it more like the one they loved in the
Southwest. "We have basically been trying to see if we couldn't
light a fire under this church ever since," he says. They speak of
their congregation as "a mission field." In order to find the spiritual encouragement that they need for this "mission work," Bill
and his wife often travel forty-five minutes on Saturday nights to
attend a nondenominational megachurch. Bill says that they go
there to "get our batteries charged and then we come back to the
mission field and try to pass along the spirit." The spiritual energy
they experience in this other worship setting gives the assurance
that Bill and his wife need. Armed with assurance that their faith
makes sense, they return to their own congregation with energy to
try to help it to be more faithful.

When speaking of his faith Bill often uses the phrase "makes
sense." His dissatisfaction with his current congregation centers
around its unwillingness to talk about what he considers the core
issue for Christians: the choice of whether to spend eternity with
God or in hell. He remembers teaching youth: "We were clear to
the kids that there is going to be a hell and that it is eternal. And
that your destination is your choice." Bill identified scripture as a

primary source for this core issue. "Eventually it does come down to either you believe that what God has written in the Bible is true, or you don't." While Bill reads the Bible with critical and historical tools, the promises of scripture that we can choose eternal life are the lens through which he understands the biblical message. These promises in scripture assure Bill of the validity of his beliefs.

A scientist, Bill finds his faith confirmed by his experiences of nature and the order of the world.

> Tell me that you can look at a field of flowers or the birds of the air; tell me that you can look at God's creation and not understand that there is some rationality to this. In fact, an intelligent power must be behind all of this and orchestrating all of this. And if that's the case, explain to me how having an intelligent being that he's created simply die and turn into dust and nothing happen makes any sense at all. God did not give us the kinds of depth of soul; he didn't give us the kind of being that he gave us to turn us back into dust. That does not make sense.

Bill finds assurance in the evidence that his scientific mind sees in the universe and in logic and its congruence with the witness of the Judeo-Christian tradition. In addition, Bill honors the "three-thousand-year-old system that [God] put in place and documented." The documentation of God's promise, found in scripture and in creation, provides the assurance that directs Bill's life.

Bill's certainty has not made him arrogant. He is quick to recognize that he is privileged, but he doesn't attribute the privilege to God. Instead, he recognizes that privilege is more a function of his social position as a white, middle-class person in the United States. What he attributes to God is his ability to appreciate and enjoy life more. "I can turn lemons into lemonade easier because I think I do understand what life is about, what is important and what is not." Understanding what life is about has given Bill the assurance upon which he has built his life and faith. Further assurance is provided by God's presence in his life. Experiences of the empowerment of the Holy Spirit have contributed to Bill's sense of certainty and order. He says, "There are occasions where I know that something inside of me is beyond my own capacity. A thousand different things have happened right in my life, for which I give God the glory."

Christian faith makes sense to Bill and provides a clear guide for life.

> You can be filled with the Holy Spirit, and because of that, you can be empowered to do things that you would otherwise not expect to be able to do. If you accept that idea and give it a try, then you find out that it is really true. Then that [realization] empowers you to do even more. And all of a sudden you know, yep, this is what life is about.

Bill testified powerfully to the certainties upon which his life is built, but he hastened to admit that he still struggles. He could not claim to have "all the answers." Even so, he could put his confidence in God's plan. For Bill, the basics are belief that God is the creator, that God has put all of creation in place, and that God has a plan for each person's life.

> You may not have the plan, but he has the plan. And once you get past that, everything else is a minor detail. I'm going to continue to seek, but I know God is in control and that he wants me to do the best that I can to help others figure that out. Then things start to fall into place. Things start to make sense.

Bill relies upon God's plan for his life. He is sure that there is a plan. That belief gives his life meaning.

### REFLECTION

*Perhaps you have found a promise in the Bible that offers "Blessed Assurance." What is that promise? Find it and refresh your memory. Now retell it in your own words. How is it your story?*

## Yearning for Assurance

Terri satisfied her yearning for assurance by deciding to be a Christian disciple. Bill satisfied his yearning by comparing the truths of the Christian tradition with the truths he observed in a Christian community and in nature. Monty cast aside his childhood faith as he tried to make sense of the complexity and ambiguity he experienced in Vietnam. But he returned to a place of assurance when he revisited the spiritual dimension of life and found God there.

Some of the people you met in earlier chapters also yearn for certainty and order, but they may express it differently. They want to be sure that they are living in accordance with God's plan or leading. And they want to find a way to make it all make sense.

Eleanor, for instance, who wanted to know what she was supposed to do, yearned for assurance around issues of vocation. Unlike Eleanor, Bill is confident that he is doing what God wants him to do. Bill has found the certainty for which Eleanor yearns. Claude would describe the basics of Christian faith in terms similar to Bill's language about God's plan for eternal life, but Claude yearns to find the confident comfort that Bill exhibits.

For Sophia and Frederick, both wise and thoughtful people who have lived many years, assurance requires accepting change and revision in one's understanding of faith. Sophia, like Bill, looks for how the Bible and the Christian tradition connect with her life experiences. However, unlike Bill, Sophia has not found congruence everywhere. She sees the Bible as a book that raises questions rather than giving answers. And she does not expect everyone to find the same answers. "You don't have to put it all together and sum it up nicely and make one statement that is going to cover everybody's opinion." Sophia learned from her family that God's love is certain. That truth has enabled her to value questions above answers and ambiguity above certainty.

Frederick too has been a searcher and learner all his life. Like Sophia and Bill, he seeks to confirm truths that he gathers from life with the wisdom of the Bible and Christian tradition. When he sees them fitting together, he has what he calls an "insight." Frederick describes his search:

> The more I have thought, studied, and read, the more that Christian theology makes rational sense to me. If we can't explain the universe in theological terms, we have no explanation except science, and that's not much of an explanation. So it really all comes down to how we take teachings out of the Bible and apply them to real life.

Frederick trusts God even as he searches for understanding. "Sometimes I think I begin to see little inklings, and I believe the answer is out there; I just haven't found the key to it." For Frederick, the search is fruitful and joyous because of God's presence in the process. "As long as I can remember, I have felt a power in my life which I now feel is the Holy Spirit." Frederick is confident that the insights are "out there." He experiences assurance as he searches for them, yet he is still puzzled about why the searching doesn't always "produce a lot of answers." He wonders, "Does this lack of discoveries, insights, or revelations mean that we did not recognize the revelations that were present, that there were not any, or that we just settled for the old, existing patterns?" He believes that our holding on to the assurance of existing patterns often keeps us from seeing the revelations out there. He finds assurance in a trusting search for a God of grace and meaning.

## REFLECTION

*When have you let go of an old answer so that a new insight could take hold? From what assumptions did this letting-go process free you? Toward what realizations did it move you?*

Franz, the German American we met in chapter 5, struggled for many years because he could not see how to connect his work in the world of finance with his faith. "I labored for the longest time under strange division between the church, where God is, and the rest of the world." But Franz finally came to see that there is no division. He recognizes that he is in ministry everywhere when he interacts in loving, Christian ways. He affirmed that this understanding of all life together had relieved a great deal of tension. He found assurance that all his life was lived in communion with God. People often struggle with an open question for many years. When the insight finally comes that resolves the question, they find certainty and order. Life finally makes sense.

For Thomas, whose education included both science and the law, assurance came through an opportunity to join a book group in his church where theological questions were raised. In this group, at age sixty-six, Thomas finally found a place where he could articulate a theology in his language. He has come to understand that the languages of science and the law are different from the language of faith. This insight has allowed Thomas to embrace the emotional certainty of metaphors from the Bible.

Thomas met Brother James through a series of coincidences because they share the same last name. Brother James believes Christ spoke to him and told him to love everyone and not to be afraid. As a result, he goes out on the streets at night looking for trouble. Often the trouble is gang members seeking revenge for some act. He stands between the killers and their targets. "I get in the car and I drive down. I wear the robe of a brother so they can tell who I am. They know why I'm there—that I will offer my life.

I think that is what makes them feel that at least somebody thinks they are worth dying for." Thomas was very moved by meeting Brother James. "I've never met anybody before who said [he] had spoken to Christ. I don't think it is true in either the scientific or legal sense, but it is certainly true to Brother James, and his commitment makes it true to me."

"His commitment makes it true to me." After so many years of struggling to make sense of faith with the rules of evidence from science and the law, Thomas has found the language of faith in the life and witness of Brother James. This example provides the assurance for which Thomas has yearned.

## REFLECTION

*Have you known someone whose commitment "made it true" to you? Think about how that commitment affected you. Have you thanked that person for his or her witness? What effect has that witness had on your life?*

Thomas also experienced a blessed assurance he received while visiting a large cathedral in Europe. As he walked around in the cathedral, he thought he heard a choir.

There were six or seven people standing at the back, and there was one young man standing at the acoustical center of this space. I'd seen him come in with a little boy and a friend about the same age. The acoustics multiplied his voice and the overtones, and everything reverberated. It sounded like a choir. It was extraordinary. And everybody standing there was just awed by this sacred music in this sacred place. Everybody was in tears. All of us were touched by this music, in that place, without any adornment, without language. It was all poetry. None of us knew one another, and we would never see one another again, but we shared this capacity for a sense of the sacred.

Thomas has found a way to put aside his legal and scientific lenses and to allow the truth of this experience of the sacred to be certain for him. He lives with the assurance for which we all yearn.

## REFLECTION

*When have you experienced a holy moment? What did it teach you about God? about life? about yourself?*

# Thrashing in the Night

Wilma, Thomas, and Christine gathered in conversation around a table in a church parlor when Wilma described the search to know God's acceptance, God's truth, and the faithfulness of her vocation as "thrashing in the night." The others immediately agreed with that image. They all knew nights filled with fear, concern, and struggle to accept, understand, or know what to do. They all prayed through these nights, sometimes with clarity resulting, other times with just thrashing. Wilma described the experience: "To me it's our struggle with accepting the mystery. That our deepest understanding of God comes down to the mystery and the grace that enters in as the center of our being." She concludes, "There is mystery that we can't unravel, so as we try to accept it, we thrash."

Christine adds, "For me it's like wrestling. I'm taking this idea and I'm trying to beat it down, trying to get past it, trying to wrestle with it." Later she told us that when she said those words, she was in the midst of a personal crisis of loss. She was trying to understand the loss; she was wrestling with it, struggling to express a reality that was tearing her apart. The conversation itself and the community of seekers were what she needed. Together they provided an opportunity to be upheld in the midst of focused theological reflection about life.

Christianity offers a language that sometimes differs from everyday language. Just as the languages of law, medicine, engineering, and sports differ and help us see and focus on particular aspects of life, so the language of religion is the language of "connection to the universe," as Thomas phrases it.

> All human beings I've ever met have a need to work out their connection with the universe, birth and death, and all the other suffering they experience and cause others. That's a language that is traditionally the language of sacred texts—there theology is talking about beginnings and endings, and there's dealing with suffering, and with the primal milestones of human life.

Thomas adds, "There is a vast community of human beings who share these kinds of questions and thoughts." He fears that too often the natural ways institutions seek to hold onto their own realities blind us to the new work that God is doing in our midst. Institutional thinking is also often afraid of the questioning because it is "afraid of the possibility of unraveling."

Yet the questioning and the thrashing are precisely what need to happen. Thomas calls us to open the doors and windows for "a revival of religious thinking"—to honor the complexity and depth of the issues themselves. Easy answers will fail. All the persons we interviewed believe we need groups that honor and allow the thrashing, drawing on the depth and complexity of religious language, as well as seeking to express it in ways that embody assurance. We can trust because we have met a God who first trusted and accepted us.

Christine states her need for a community that helps her connect her vocation with what "goes on day to day." Without such a community of grace, reflection, and faith, we "hit a wall and try to find our way around." The disciples on the road to Emmaus drew on all of the traditions and beliefs their community had given them. They also drew on their years of experience with Jesus. As they gathered around the table that evening, they became aware of

God's presence. They understood the death of Jesus in a whole new way and ran back to Jerusalem to proclaim and carry out their vocations. In this Bible story we recognize our own experiences in the experiences of the disciples.

Here is how Thomas describes the importance of community: "There are lots of people exploring and faithfully attempting to keep the faith—to translate the meaning of religious experience into languages consistent with the other languages we have to deal with every day. I personally think that this is not only possible but marvelous." He summarizes what he experiences in his community of faith: "I share this mystery of existence—it's very exciting. I find my experience of coming here [to the interview] marvelously deepening and broadening. Every day it [the Christian life] is a very integrated kind of experience."

Thomas experiences a caring community, emotional connection, and intellectual concern for living and understanding.

## REFLECTION

*When have you experienced a community that allowed you to wrestle with faith questions? What can you do to offer such an experience to others?*

The search for assurance is best engaged in a faith community that

- knows the traditions and willingly wrestles with them,
- believes God actively works in people's lives,
- seeks to support one another with care,
- gathers around the welcome table where God is present, seeking guidance.

As a result of a community that seeks assurance together, Thomas claims, "My faith deepens my connection with other human beings and with God, the creator of the universe."

As we engage in the questions and search for assurance, we can affirm with the hymn writer:

This is my story, this is my song,
Praising my Savior all the day long.

For God is present in the search, offering blessed assurance.

# 7

## YEARNING TO BE KNOWN AND ACCEPTED

We yearn for assurance that we are on the right track; we wonder whether we can trust in our sense of what is meaningful and good. We yearn for assurance that God enfolds our lives with love and guidance. By the grace of God we are children and heirs of salvation. But more than assurance that we are living faithfully and that God knows and accepts us, we seek to be known and accepted in the congregation where we worship and serve.

Sophia sounded the same note several times as she spoke of her life: "I need to be in a community of people who are trying to live as God wants them to and who come not because they are perfect but because they are seeking, yearning like I am." On the outside, Sophia appears to have it all together. She is tall, elegant, well-groomed, and articulate. Her congregation respects her because she has held various offices and helped make many decisions in the life of the church. Sunday school classes seek her out as their teacher. We met her in chapter 4 as she struggled with pain and disability that left her angry with God. We read about her again in chapter 6 and learned about her certainty of the value of questions and searching. She says,

> I think the church ought to be a place where I'm free to ask my questions even if they sound dumb. It needs to be a place where I am accepted no matter what I think, with room for me to grow in my struggle. And I have changed what I think many times. Forty-two years in this church, and about every ten years I look back and say, "I used to think that? Oh, my gosh!" And in the next ten years I hope I'm going to do some more changing, but I want to be free to change and still be accepted as a person.

On one level, Sophia certainly is accepted and valued in her congregation. However, she is uncertain that they accept her for who she is. She is certain of her acceptance as a leader, teacher, and guide for the administration of the church. Yet she is uncertain that her community of faith could accept her if they genuinely knew her. Acceptance without genuine knowing does not satisfy her. Acceptance and following the truth as we see it with integrity sometimes work against each other.

## The Conflict of Being Known and Being Accepted

Sophia has yearned for acceptance for much of her life, although she often made choices and held onto convictions she identified as different from those prevailing in her community and culture. Because her father died when she was a toddler, Sophia grew up in an all-female household. Her mother moved with Sophia and her two older sisters to live near her parents. The whole extended family participated in the little church that was part of a rural circuit with five congregations.

Sophia describes her grandfather as a pillar of the congregation. "My grandfather always did the Wednesday night prayer meeting, and every last one of his nine grandchildren were there. So I grew up in the church." Her grandfather owned a store and also raised peaches and cattle. Her oldest sister was disabled by polio. Her mother taught school. Times were hard.

One of Sophia's earliest memories reflects her desire to be both known and accepted. The incident occurred when Sophia was about seven years old. She and her first cousin had gotten into an argument on the school playground.

> She turned to me and put her hands on her hips and said, "Well, I know something you don't." I looked at her funny and she said, "Our grandmother is my grandmother, but she's not your grandmother. She is my grandmother, real, true grandmother, and if you don't believe me, go home and ask your momma." I just felt like the earth had come crushing down on me because I adored my grandmother. I knew my mother's mother had died when she was born, but the word *step* had never been used.
>
> Immediately after school I went straight to my grandmother's house, and I burst in. I remember saying to her, "Well, are you my grandmother or not?" My grandmother was unflappable. "What kind of foolishness is that? Of course I'm your real grandmother," she said. "But I'll tell you what. Let's go in the kitchen and raid the cookie jar and go out on the back steps, and while we munch our cookies I want to tell you a story about that." So we did.
>
> She began, "Now, you know your mother's mother died when she was born." And I said yes, Momma had told us that. And she said, "Well, then, your grandfather came a-courting, and he asked me to marry him. I chose to marry him. The first thing he wanted me to do was to see his darling little brown-eyed girl whose name was

Mary. I fell in love with her. Then I chose to marry your grandfather, and when I chose to marry him, I chose your mother as my daughter."

Then she said, "Sophia, you have to understand there are two ways we get babies. One is we 'born' them, and one is we choose them. I chose your mother, and that is the very special way of having children. And I chose you for my granddaughter." I remember she munched a cookie for a minute and then she looked at me and said, "So don't ever let anybody tell you any different because we know better, don't we?" And she reached over and hugged me. A weight was lifted from my shoulders. I never again worried about it because she had given me a gift of belonging when I was afraid I did not belong.

In the midst of this delightful story is the germ of a yearning that has remained important for Sophia throughout her life. "I knew what it meant to belong. I learned that from my grandmother. I know how everybody needs to belong. I think that is what gets kids in trouble a lot of times."

Sophia's keen intelligence and strong streak of individualism worked against the comfort of belonging. She continually stretched social conventions with her efforts to choose her own path. She also asked questions that were different from others' questions. Fiercely independent and occasionally rebellious, Sophia recalls a time when she confessed that she had gotten in trouble for asking so many questions and challenging her Sunday school teacher. Her mother counseled her to save the questions and ask them at home. Sophia has struggled to understand the Bible all her life and has concluded, "The Bible questions us. Instead of turning to the Bible to find answers, we look for the essential questions."

Sophia grew up in a small town, nurtured by the church and her extended family. Her mother was independent as well. Sophia recalls a summer when some African-American women asked her mother to help them put on a vacation Bible school for their children. Although none of the other white women in town would help, Sophia's mother did. She explained, "I don't really care what anybody thinks. They asked for help, and they need help, so I'm going." Sophia's mother modeled independent thinking and self-reliance.

## REFLECTION

*Recall a time when you had questions of faith as a child. How did you address the questions? In whom could you confide?*

Bright and accomplished, Sophia left for a women's college when she was only sixteen. There she began bumping up against rules she regarded as oppressive. For example, the students were required to go to church every Sunday, but Sophia considered the Methodist preacher long-winded and boring. When she found out that the Roman Catholic priest delivered a short homily at Mass, she signed up to attend there. For a small-town Methodist girl in 1934, that was quite adventuresome. Protestants and Catholics kept separate in most towns. But Sophia was undeterred. Ready for whatever came along, she moved after graduation to the largest city in her state and got a job teaching school.

Eventually, Sophia married and had two children. She remembers many struggles as she and her husband learned how to negotiate their differences. She returned to teaching after taking a few years off while the children were young. Her husband resisted this; they didn't need the income. But Sophia persisted and taught sixth and seventh grade for many years. For a Southern woman during the 1950s and '60s, that was an unusual choice.

Two other important incidents illustrate Sophia's independence. She was part of a Sunday school class that came under fire from others in her church. They accused the teacher of subversiveness and asked the pastor to "silence" this teacher. Sophia acknowledged that this teacher was "always going to be the basis of some dissension in the church because she opens doors for people that nobody else opens. And it's wonderful!" All of her life Sophia had yearned for someone to allow her to open those doors. The class was important as Sophia claimed her place to stand. The teacher's acceptance of Sophia's theological explorations made it possible for her to risk. The controversy over the class occurred at the same time racial integration was looming. The white congregation resisted integration, but a man who coached a church league team had an integrated team. Sophia recalls,

> The coach said to me, "Do you think it would be okay for some of these black kids who play basketball to come to church with some of the rest of the team?" And I said, "I think it would be wonderful." He said, "Would you sit with them?" and I said, "Sure." They came, and I sat on the pew right behind them because they filled up a pew. And I stopped and talked to all of them and got two or three people I knew to sit on the pew right behind them because I was afraid it was going to be vacant in front and vacant behind, and I didn't want that to happen. That was the first integration in this church.

This incident occurred in the wake of an executive committee decision that two stewards would take any African-Americans who tried to attend worship to the minister's office and "keep them busy talking while the church service was going on so there wouldn't be any trouble." Instead, Sophia independently acted on her principles, and the church experienced its first integrated worship service. This act of justice set Sophia apart from many in her congregation who resented her role in the incident. People admired her courage but found themselves uncomfortable around her, further setting her apart from the very place where she longed to be accepted.

Even today Sophia continues to encourage and support voices that raise difficult questions, that help us encounter issues and tell the truth. Recently she helped sponsor a conversation on homosexuality, relationships, and families in her church. The pastor was reluctant to raise controversial issues, but Sophia persisted. "It's time for us to talk about these things in the church!" she declared.

## REFLECTION

*Are you aware of topics that should be addressed in light of our faith that have not been included at your church because of their controversial nature? What could you do to encourage your education leaders to plan opportunities for theological reflection about these issues?*

# The Church As a Place of Belonging

Sophia identified "Christian community, belonging" as a recurrent theme in her life, yet she consistently critiqued cultural and religious values. This critique often set her apart from the very community in which she longed to be accepted. Thus she stated with conviction, "I need to be in a community of people who try to live as God wants them to and who come not because they are perfect but because they are seeking, yearning like I am." Sometimes the church has satisfied this yearning for Sophia; at times it has failed.

## REFLECTION

*When have you taken a stand that separated you from a community? Did you find acceptance in another community as you took that unpopular stand?*

Some of us struggle through youth, being bullied or teased. Hilary, an African-American in her early forties, begins her life story with the words, "As a child, I didn't like myself." Middle school was an especially difficult time for her.

The kids would just pick and mess with me. I was very small. The kids never used my name. They called me "big nose." Middle school was the worst time in my life. I got turned on to the idea to go to church. If anybody would accept you for what you are, it would be people that were in a church because they could see through the nose, they could see through the color, they could see through a lot of things, and they could help you too. I went to different churches, but I never really got what I was looking for.

Hilary endured many difficult times, but she put herself through school and now has a career in education. She made mistakes but affirms God's presence in her life. "I feel God's guidance every day of my life. I don't only feel his guidance. There is a path for me."

Hilary knows that sometimes she overextends herself. "That's the human side of me, wanting to do everything and help everybody, and I can't do that." But her spiritual side reaches out even when she is not aware of it, she believes. When church leaders or pastors say, "Hilary did this or Hilary helped with that," her name has been mentioned. "I may not have even felt like I've touched those people's lives, but I have because of my name being mentioned, whereas as a child my name was never spoken. My name itself tells me that I am special."

Now she says she has "a second chance." She recognizes that money or possessions are not important. "I would rather be full on the spirit of God than to be full on anything that anybody has." Hilary has found a place where people know her name. Nose and color and possessions don't matter. She is accepted.

## REFLECTION

*Hearing your name spoken aloud is a primary sign that you are known. If you are a parent, recall the process of choosing a name for your child. How did you hope that name would affect his or her character? What story lies behind your name?*

Hilary affirms, "God has a place for me, and God works through me all the time." Helping with a program for young children, Hilary sees God at work through her. "I knew them from the time they were babies. I see this light, you know, when the children come in and they start smiling. I really believe that smile is for me when they come through that door. When they see me, it's okay." She looks pleased but wistful as she adds, "I have always wanted to feel like that. I found a hiding place in this congregation."

## REFLECTION

*Are you still looking for a "hiding place" where you smile as you come in the door? When have you allowed God to work through you to help others feel comfortable when they come into the church building?*

Fran didn't have to deal with racial discrimination like Hilary, but she too experienced a painful adolescence. She never felt accepted by her peers. Overweight and religious, she just didn't fit in. "I've always had a sense of being different from everyone because I can remember believing very strongly in God as a child. I've always felt connected." Even so, her early years were painful. She could claim the pain now. Remembering it has brought clarity about her ministry. Fran is committed to providing a place for children and youth to feel accepted, including

> a young man who is rejected everywhere—at school, in his own family, and certainly here at church. It's a huge conflict because there are a couple [of] families that don't want this child around their child. I've had numerous requests to remove him from the youth program altogether. Well, never, ever am I going to do that. All this child knows is being rejected, and I feel so strongly about that because church needs to be the one place where you can come and feel acceptance. So that's something that I've refused to do, and I'm not popular among a few people because of that.

Fran's commitment to acceptance has made her vulnerable to rejection. What Fran has yearned for all her life—acceptance—is a gift she tries to offer others.

## REFLECTION

*Where have you taken a stand for acceptance? When has this stand caused you to risk being rejected? What do you suppose God would think about it?*

In chapter 6 we met Monty, who went through a period of intense cynicism and then found a way to reclaim the assurance for which he yearned. He explains, "I really did not like the things that I saw in society, and religion, and everything else. I didn't lose my religion. I lost my willingness to deal with churches and even name what my religion was." At fifty, Monty has rediscovered the value of Christian community. He is willing to invest himself in a process of listening and recognizes the value of a small group in supporting that process. But he still insists that there must be an authentic community where he can be genuinely known. He decries the unspoken taboos on some subjects that he finds in his congregation. He wants to be able to make his religion relevant to all aspects of life, including his sexuality. "My sexuality is a part of me. I come to the church door as me. If you can't accept that, then I have a problem." If it is to feel genuine, acceptance must include being known.

## REFLECTION

*What parts of your life do you not discuss at church? What are the taboo topics in your congregation? Do you believe that your church would not welcome certain parts of you? What would it mean to be able to think theologically about those hidden parts of your life?*

Seventeen-year-old Emily, who found a church that gave her "room to breathe," expressed a similar yearning. She spent her earliest years in a succession of congregations that "drilled religion into her head." When she and her mother found a congregation that "didn't push anything on you," she began to discover her own yearnings and to welcome opportunities for spiritual growth. Emily felt accepted in this congregation. She could participate in decision-making processes and was trusted to teach young children. Yet she welcomed the "room to breathe" that accepted her youthful search for a faith that she could make her own.

Thomas spent much of his life yearning to address the suffering and evil of the death camps in World War II. He had little confidence in the church's ability to deal with such profound sin. Some of the lack of confidence was due to an experience he had in confirmation class as an adolescent. He asked a question about the divinity of Christ. "I was not a critic of the church but a curious boy," he explains. The pastor jumped on Thomas and told him his question was inappropriate.

> I learned I had stepped way outside the bounds. I wanted to be part of this group. My friends were a part of this group, and my dad was on the church board. My mother was a lovely person, and she was embarrassed. So I just shut up. I felt bad about asking the question, and it seemed to me I transgressed somewhere. I didn't understand what was so bad about it.

Nearly sixty years after the incident, Thomas recalled this story with puzzlement and hurt. He chose acceptance over an honest search for faith, but this choice was painful. Parenthetically, Thomas was not alone. We were surprised by the number of persons who remembered childhood experiences of being silenced in the church or of being questioned severely. These childhood recollections remain formative for adults many years later. Persons who were rebuffed as children often find it difficult to feel welcome or to be vulnerable and open in a congregation.

## REFLECTION

*What childhood experiences of church do you remember? How much does your congregation emphasize children's ministries? What is the mission of your church's programs for children?*

Indeed, we yearn for acceptance in our congregation. But that acceptance is meaningful only when we feel genuinely known. We need to be allowed to search for God in ways that fit our particular questions and yearnings. In addition, we yearn to know that God accepts us and knows us. Like the psalmist, we cry, "Search me . . . and know my heart" (Ps. 139:23).

# 8

---

# YEARNING FOR THE
# NEW CREATION

---

The yearning to be known and accepted by both our congregations and God is strong, as are the yearnings for meaning,
healing, and justice. For many people, the longing for meaning,
healing, and justice expands to encompass more and more of the
world. We yearn for the kind of community to which the life of
Jesus pointed. We yearn for peace with justice. When we encounter
people and cultures different from our own, we yearn to find commonalities and to accept differences. The differences help us see
the limits in our own perspectives. Then we yearn for a real "welcome table" where people from north, south, east, and west come
together in hope, nourishing one another and working to build
the structures and relationships of community.

The writer of Revelation describes his vision of a new heaven
and a new earth.

"See, the home of God is among mortals.
He will dwell with them as their God;
they will be his peoples,
and God himself will be with them;

he will wipe every tear from their eyes.
Death will be no more;
mourning and crying and pain will be no more,
for the first things have passed away."
—Revelation 21:3-4

The vision of the new creation, like the one found in Isaiah 25:6-9 and 65:16-25, describes a community that transcends boundaries and embraces all people. The vision calls us to build a community with God and with one another that embodies a new creation. The new creation expands to all peoples—new wine, rich food, loving relationships, the honoring of traditions, and community across differences united in the grace of God. Community grows out of our quest to fulfill this vision in light of God's grace. Community does not result from our similarity or commonality. God's community transcends boundaries and is a new creation.

## Communing with the Other

We met Thomas in chapter 5 as he described a lifetime devoted to addressing suffering and evil. He was alienated from the Christian church because of its inability to confront evil in significant ways and because the church too often continued to perpetuate evil. Thomas also did not feel that the church welcomed his questions of faith. What brought him back to the church was a surprising encounter with Buddhism in a Japanese hotel while on a business trip.

In the hotels in Japan they have the Buddhist equivalent of the Gideon Bible. I began to read about Buddhism and found it fascinating. It dealt with suffering and the way to reduce suffering. It had a rational appeal to it. And it was a beginning for me of trying to interpret Christianity.

Here Thomas discovered a religion's direct effort to engage suffering—a concern that had motivated him since he was an eighteen-year-old soldier in Europe. His adolescent experiences in the Christian church had not encouraged him to search for understanding of suffering. The Buddhist concern for suffering led him back to his own faith tradition, looking again for how Christianity deals with the meaning of suffering.

Again the answer was surprising. What he found especially arresting gave him an insight about the saying attributed to Jesus: "Turn the other cheek." As a boy he recalled struggling with that teaching. "I couldn't turn the other cheek. If somebody hurt me, I felt angry with [that person]." A similar story from Buddhism helped Thomas to look freshly at what Jesus meant:

> Buddha, in his teaching years, was walking down a road, and he came upon a man coming the other way. The man saw him and for some reason was angry with him and abused him terribly—yelling at him and threatening him. Buddha listened, and he said, "Pardon me, my friend. May I interrupt you and ask you a question?" And the man replied, "Well, all right." Buddha said, "If one person offers another a gift, but it is refused, who owns the gift?" And the man said, "Well, it is obvious. Until the gift is accepted, it is still owned by the person offering it." And Buddha said, "So it is with abuse. Good day."

Thomas found that this explanation, from a religion not his own, helped him reexamine the faith tradition he had found inadequate and see it more clearly. "It made sense—leaving the anger with the person sending it to you." The insight helped Thomas to look again at the teaching of Christ. "Maybe that is what Christ meant," he said. He found the insight by listening to and incorporating wisdom from another religion into his own. He broadened his vision. He experienced a deep connection with a culture that had seemed incomprehensible to his Western values. The God of creation and grace who wants suffering to be defeated surrounded him. He experienced, even if only in a moment, the hope of God's new creation.

## REFLECTION

*When have you experienced or learned a truth completely outside traditional Christian sources that helped you make sense of your faith? How did the insight come? What effect did this discovery have on your sense of connection to people who practice that faith?*

Thomas's search for answers and insights for his own faith has provided impetus for him to explore other cultures. Nevertheless, he has continued to be an active member of a mainstream Protestant congregation in middle America. He recognizes the value of difference and seeks opportunities to connect to difference in order to learn more about himself. In his own community, he works to heal Jewish and Christian relationships. He helps create opportunities for Jews and Christians to come together, to remember, and to grieve. Then together, they can forgive and move forward. They can move out into the world as a healing presence, agents of the new creation.

Encounters with difference often provide opportunities to learn about ourselves. When a church group plans a mission trip to help people in need, they often focus on what help they can offer, such as collecting boxes of clothing or eyeglasses to give away. They may offer medical assistance, labor, or consultation to people whose lives are disrupted by disaster or who are caught in a cycle of poverty. Such volunteer groups can accomplish much good. However, the mission trip is often most powerful when it helps volunteers examine their own lives and values. They return realizing how privileged they are. And the privilege does not reside in wealth and education alone, for the very fact of meeting and connecting deeply with other humans who offer gifts of grace as they receive is a privilege. Volunteers often find more gracious hospitality among the poor than they practice themselves. They may become critical of their own assumptions about what is really important in life. As they make meaningful connections across the gulf of differences, they experience glimpses of the new creation.

## REFLECTION

*What unexpected values have you learned from persons of different faith, cultures, or socioeconomic levels?*

## Risking for the Other

Sheryl grew up in an affluent, homogeneous community. Status was important. Wearing the right clothes and dating the right guys were primary values during her high school years. However, she was not satisfied with that narrow range of acceptance. When she went to a large university, she found the diversity stimulating. "We didn't know who was who!" she recalls. Without the usual "score sheet" for status with points for where you lived, who your parents were, and to which country club you belonged, people could be accepted for who they were. "I learned at this university," she says, "that I can like people who are different from me." Like many young people away from home for the first time, Sheryl reveled in the new freedom to learn about other values and other cultural practices. "What I needed to do was to open myself up to other people who didn't necessarily think or act like I did or even want to be like me. That was a rejoicing. It was confirmation of what had been going on inside me." She caught a glimpse of the new creation and found it liberating.

Sheryl now belongs to a congregation known for its diversity. People gather on Sunday and discuss events from their lives and efforts of service. These people pray together as they yearn for God and for faithful lives. They want to help one another make a difference. The pastor even ends every worship service with the words: "Leave here. Take it to the streets!" They work for a new creation.

Delia also has caught a glimpse of the new creation. Delia's life story illustrates how encounters with difference can provide opportunities to incorporate broader values and perspectives. Her childhood was preparation. She grew up in a large Southern city. Her mother was divorced. The Depression years were difficult, and her small family often had to live with other people. "You had this mix of families living together. You had to adjust to that kind of situation." As a young child, Delia experienced differences in those families and learned to accept persons whose values and practices differed from the ones by which she and her mother lived. In fact, simply to get along, she had to learn to accept difference and find points of connection.

The anchor in the constant moving and struggling to keep the family together was the church. Two memories of the church stand out for Delia. One is of a man from the church coming up the stairs to the flat where the family lived, bringing a basket of food. "That really stuck with me," affirms Delia. "Those people seemed to care for us." The church also welcomed her as an adolescent. "They really got a good youth group going. It was a wonderful experience." The church community welcomed and cared for Delia's family. No status was expected. Need overcame expectations.

## REFLECTION

*How do you view status? Where does it fit into the social structures of your congregation? How does your understanding of your social status affect the way you relate to others in your congregation? How do the teachings and life of Jesus speak to these issues?*

Delia was married at eighteen and spent two years alone while her young husband served in the Pacific theater during World War II. "It was a lonely time," she remembers, yet the community of

the church continued to be a place of belonging and support. After
the war, Delia and her husband moved several times. Each time the
church was "home and family" for Delia.

However, the church was under tremendous pressure to
change. Both the church and the surrounding culture struggled
with efforts to include women and to end segregation. Delia was
caught up in those movements. She became one of the first two
women elected to the administrative council of her congregation
in 1964. "They took an old one and a young one. I was the young
one then," she says with a smile. She was a natural choice, she believes. "I haven't been seen as a threat because I'm a married
woman with children. I go along with the [traditional] woman's
role. I'm safe." Delia did not depart from her culture's role expectation for women, but she moved beyond the norms by offering
hospitality to those on the margins, working in her denomination's peace mission, inviting new ideas, and remaining open to
God's revelation in broader ways.

Delia continued her deep involvement in many phases of the
church over the next forty years. Her involvement brought her in
contact with people and cultures different from her own. She explained, "Opportunities to speak out become compelling when I
know what is going on. I go to all kinds of conferences and get exposed to [ideas] that are out there."

When we interviewed Delia, she had attended the controversial
Re-imagining Conference, a gathering of Christian women in
Minneapolis, Minnesota, that explored theology and worship practice. A firestorm of criticism occurred in her denomination after that
conference. Because she had attended, Delia found herself listening to
people who were angry, frightened, and condemning. She was able
to accept their "real feeling of threat." In fact, her ministry began by
allowing others to express their fears without her overreacting to or
denying those fears. Humbly she witnessed to them of the power of
the conference and its rituals for her own faith. Delia realized, "I
could not deny my own experience because it is real; it's valid."

Her commitment "to honor other people's experiences" meant that she and others could engage in honest conversations and build bridges, rather than engage in conflict born of fear. In the wake of the Re-imagining Conference, many voices shouted that the theological expressions that were part of the conference were all wrong. Delia responded to those voices: "Wait a minute. [These theological explorations] drive us back to saying, 'What do I really believe?' We must be able to answer that question but also not discount different answers."

The network and educational opportunities that Delia enjoyed due to her involvement with her denomination were a source of learning. "The wider the range of experiences you get, the more open you are to more experiences. Plus, you may lead the way for some other people, showing them the way to go." Learning about poverty, the injustices of systems, and the needs of the entire human family had empowered Delia to speak out and help others see the needs. She worked for justice where she saw it was lacking.

But more than that, she had the opportunity to experience a wider faith community. Delia believes that "we're all in this together. We're all human beings with foibles and problems." A grandmother who has been married to the same man for over fifty years, Delia has ventured into the unknown and found people there that God loves. God's hospitality to her empowers her to extend hospitality to others. Knowing that, she yearns for the new creation where "mourning and crying and pain will be no more" (Rev. 21:4) and where God will dwell with us.

### REFLECTION

*What experiences of different people or different cultures have you had that helped you envision the new creation?*

## Embodying the New Creation

The people Penny encounters in her vocation are different. Their difference is not cultural but physical; she works with children with profound intellectual disabilities who are medically fragile. Often they cannot talk and are unable to leave the hospital. Penny admits that she develops an intense relationship with the parents of these children. Because of the children's profound limitations and because their life spans are often shortened, the parents express that "they hate God, and they question God and wonder what's going on." Without her faith she could not do this work, she is sure. The future is limited for these children.

> People say, "What's this child even doing here?" Or "You're not doing a thing for her." But I don't believe that. People think I'm absolutely nuts because I see possibilities in these children. I can see Jesus in the children. When they fight to live even though they are attached to a machine and they are basically dead, something is keeping them alive, and I feel it is God.

Penny is intensely grateful that she can leave the hospital at the end of her workday. She thanks God every day. "My job keeps me very fresh in my faith and how much I need God." For Penny, loving these fragile children is an expression of the new creation.

She told us a powerful story of a little boy who, while he could not speak, communicated with sounds. "I have this student who had a stroke when he was three. . . . He gets real excited and goes in a high octave, 'Whoop, whoop, whoop!' and rocks in his chair real hard. We can't tell what he wants." Neither Penny nor his mother understood what he meant or what excited him. Then another mother brought a recording of inspirational music into the classroom. As it started playing, the little boy began screaming, "Whoop, whoop!" Penny talked to him, and his mood changed as he felt the rhythm and tone of the music. The gospel music communicated to the little boy, and he expressed his joy. He is learning when to "whoop" loudly and when to do it softly. As Penny mentions, "I want him to be able to tell us that he is excited and really enjoying something, but at an appropriate level." Now he makes a big sound sometimes and at other times just small sounds. Even with his limits, this little boy illustrated to them that communication could take place across difference. He and those around him could understand each other and the emotions of celebration and excitement. Difference need not end community. Penny's group experienced community and caught a glimpse of the new creation where every voice and tongue is understood.

Christine, a young adult whose vocation is environmental engineering, also yearns for the new creation. She experienced a taste of it in college when she joined a coed fraternity that was a caring group of people. They all lived together in the same house and shared chores. They covenanted to support one another, to work together, and to encourage personal growth for each member. Christine describes the feeling of this group as "a real sense of equality." In this setting, "the group is more important than your own self." Christine experienced glimpses of the new creation in the fraternity, but they were only glimpses. She remembers how the group had problems with some members. "In the midst of that we were all trying to grow up and trying to figure out what to do, which made some of those times kind of difficult. We were always trying to band together to help people, which sometimes didn't work." She is not entirely naive about the difficulties of true community, whether that community consists of humans or of the entire creation. She carried that value into her work as an environmentalist. She would never want to do anything to harm the environment. The highest value is the health of the entire system, like the fraternity group. Achieving this new creation is a complicated and difficult process. But she yearns for it and actively seeks ways to work toward it.

One of the places Christine hoped to find genuine community was in an intensive Bible study group. Participation in this Bible study demands commitment to a small group, usually about twelve people, for thirty-four weeks of daily Bible reading and prayer, coupled with weekly meetings for two and a half hours. About midway through the year, Christine's group was challenged when one member revealed her homosexuality.

> She was looking for a place to call home while she was going through a very tough time, a place where she could find some support. She left the group sometime in February. That really hurt me. It really made me open my eyes and wonder what I was missing. And it made everybody in the group analyze what the group was about. And then another woman left because she felt we were tromping on the faith.

As Christine prepared to lead a group for the next year, the failure of this group weighed heavily on her mind. She did not have any easy answers for how to create true community, but she still yearned for it. Without question, the group's inability to overcome difference and hurt brought real loss. Yet, loss and hurt did not result in defeat. Christine hoped the group she was preparing to lead would converse on a deep level like her first group had done occasionally. The loss did not just engender fear; rather, it inspired her to hope and to work toward becoming an agent of conversation. Glimpses of new creation even in the midst of loss inspired efforts for new creation in a new time and place.

Many persons complete a year or more of this demanding Bible study. Often they describe the covenant group as the place where, for the first time in their lives, they learn to value difference. The groups covenant to study, pray, and gather weekly. As they come to know one another, they begin to understand the context from which each participant comes. As Christine puts it, "If this woman had a hard time that week, she doesn't need to have the group peeving at her or other interactions that aren't supportive." Christine longs to help the group welcome and include each individual while still making the work of the group the highest value.

## REFLECTION

*Have you ever participated in a small group where you could love one another and accept your differences? How did that feel? What made it possible for this openness to happen?*

## Yearning for a New Creation

The new creation is not just about feeling good; it is about justice, the interconnection of all creation, and valuing life. It is about the paradox of valuing each individual and also valuing the whole. Julia, whom we encountered in chapter 3, has a glimpse of this when she says, "My life is just an ordinary life. But everyone is special." She goes on to express the pain she feels when she sees loss, hurt, and evil in the world, and she expresses the limits she experiences in addressing it.

> I feel a lot of times that I'm not meshing with the world that I see out there. I see it as muck. I don't know how to bring a light into it sometimes. There's a lot of grit, anger, and hostility. I don't know how [to respond], besides prayers. I wish there were ways I could. And I hope the Lord will show me.

And that is just what the Lord has done. Julia lives her life as an agent of communication through literacy classes and as an agent of communion who meets real people with real needs and offers partnership and friendship. As you may remember, she adopted Mother Teresa's motto: "I don't do great things. I do small things, with great love."

Yes, Julia is an ordinary person yet at the same time is quite special. It is "one of those paradoxes that you always run into in the faith." Jesus' efforts for healing and new life occurred in concrete experiences with particular persons and families and towns. They were not great world-transforming revolutions founded in warfare and defeat of the evil and oppressive presence of Rome. Yet those small acts of love and justice began a world-transforming movement focused on offering healing and new life to creatures of God—new life and healing that became a glimpse of the hope of the new creation.

The new creation is as close and as common as a small group of humans loving one another while they deeply disagree about the mission of the church. The new creation is as huge as the entire universe. Still, we humans yearn for some connectedness to the whole. We yearn to experience a healed and reconciled community.

The yearning for a new creation is the motive that drives us to search for what we are "supposed to do." We want a vocation that will contribute. We want to know grace; we want to connect with God. This yearning drives us to find meaning in the midst of personal crisis. If we can see some larger purpose for our crisis, then the crisis is more bearable. The yearning also drives us to try to understand and alleviate suffering as we seek to make the world more just. We yearn for assurance that we are on the right track as we do what we can to participate in God's vision of the new creation.

# 9

## YEARNING FOR HOPE, YEARNING FOR GOD

The prayer Jesus taught his disciples and the one many congregations repeat every Sunday includes petitions to God:

Thy kingdom come,
Thy will be done.
Give us this day our daily bread.

Forgive us our trespasses, as we forgive those who trespass against us.

Deliver us from evil.

These petitions reflect yearnings we heard over and over in our study. The disciples with whom Jesus ministered and disciples today yearn for God's "kindom,"[1] for God's will, for God's care and sustenance, and for God's forgiveness. They yearn for the forgiveness of and a sense of community with their companions. They yearn for hope and for God's gracious presence in the midst of living.

The people who shared their lives and theological reflections with us were not strangers to loss and difficulty. They did not expect a Hollywood ending to the stories of their lives, but they displayed a resilience born of God's grace. Courage is required even to acknowledge one's yearnings for vocation, grace, meaning and healing, justice, assurance, acceptance, and participation in the new creation. Because often there are no easy answers. Because sometimes God seems silent and distant. The uncertainty of a world dominated by news of terrorism, war, and economic recession stands in stark contrast to the yearnings people express to participate in God's vision of the new creation. These faithful people were gifted with hope as they yearned for God. They committed themselves to the grace they have touched. They hope for justice, new life, and community—for God's will to be realized.

We began with Frederick's lament that "Somehow we have not made it possible for people to be theological in their daily lives." However, the stories we have told, accounts of ordinary people in ordinary congregations, belie that statement. Our interviews found people struggling faithfully to live in ways that connect them to God. We found people who were intentionally reflective about the theological implications of their life choices. Sometimes they did not have formal theological language to convey that reflection, but they searched for adequate and complex language to express the realities of their lives. They wished the church would help them more effectively gain the theological resources of their faith tradition and practice theological reflection, for they believed that remaining connected to God was an important guiding value. They knew they needed assistance to experience God's grace and understand God's call.

We have seen the rich presence of the power and grace of God in their lives. The people with whom we conversed revealed concepts of God that call us to enter into life with hope, faith, and risk. We heard great variety in ways people image God. In fact, their image of God becomes the source of hope. Therefore, in this chapter we will

explore these images, paying particular attention to how they provide hope even in the midst of suffering, fear, and uncertainty.

## REFLECTION

*Before you read about the images of God that empower these persons'
lives, tell a friend ways you image and understand God's presence in your
life. Do you consider yourself a hopeful person? Why or why not? If you
answered yes to the first question, in what ways do you express hope?*

## Hope in the Midst of Suffering and Uncertainty

Frederick's situation was surely one that could lead to despair
more easily than to hope. With his beloved wife unable to communicate and requiring round-the-clock care, his life was severely
limited. He needed to be home most of the time to feed her and
to provide other care. He had little freedom to travel to visit their
children in other cities. He faced constant uncertainty and daily re-
minders of loss. In spite of all these difficulties, he was resilient.
He struggled to describe the core that kept him going. He called it
"a deep-seated feeling that the best of good things is going to happen. Eventually, and maybe not in your lifetime, but things are
going to come out all right."

Even though Frederick's daily routine was difficult, he was
sustained by what he called "the long view." His trust in God sustained that hope. This expression did not deny the pain he faced,
nor was it an empty belief in the future; rather it was an empowering conviction that kept him engaged in life and teaching, seeking, and serving others.

For Frederick, relationships are the key elements of a meaningful
life. "First of all is your relationship to your God, through Christ, led
by the Holy Spirit; next is your relationships with others—family

first and then your community." Everything about Frederick's life reflects his attention to relationships. He continued to care for his wife when she could not give much to the relationship anymore. He remained connected to his children and their families, accepting their differences with understanding. He has taught a Sunday school class nearly every week for seventeen years and continues to prepare carefully for each week's lesson. He never misses a gathering for training of teachers. He wants to become a more skillful teacher. He reads widely and tries to relate current events to the biblical text each week. Even though the class has diminished in size and vigor as they have aged, he continues to believe in the importance of each person there. Frederick seeks to teach in ways that will both comfort and challenge these folks. His goal is to deepen faith, for himself and everyone else too. He is faithful to the task and to the members of his class.

God is the center of his life. Frederick is able to trust in that central relationship and in God's promise of salvation. He says,

> God knew when [God] created us and gave us free will that we were going to sin. God has offered to save us. [We are] like a patient with diabetes who is dying and will not take the shot of insulin that is on the table beside him. We are condemned because we reject the means of salvation.

Frederick had learned early of God's promise of salvation. He trusts in it even as he understands that the human condition includes sin. He trusts that God's grace is sufficient to enable him to trust in the ultimate promise. Even when life is limited and painful, Frederick can see the long view and feel hopeful. His view of God brings hope to Frederick.

## REFLECTION

*As you think about relationships and the ways Frederick builds and experiences them, how do you think about or image your relationship to God?*

Eleanor struggled to find the vocation that would provide the feeling of safety she'd had in earlier years when she knew she was doing what she was supposed to do. No matter what happened, she had felt secure during her tumultuous years of working in the civil rights movement. But a change of health had left her feeling unsettled and insecure. "What am I supposed to be doing?" she asked repeatedly.

A few years later, she observed the fearful reaction so many people had to the events of September 11, 2001. She affirmed that her response was more hopeful. "I don't have fear; God will take care of me. That doesn't mean I will survive other attacks; it means that whether I live or die God will take care of me. I have finally accepted that God does love me and that God is always faithful." She attributes this hopeful response to her parents and grandparents, who approached life with optimism and hope.

She admits, "As I have aged and gone through life's ups and downs, I cannot say that I have always been hopeful. I had to learn to look beyond the immediate and find God. Then I could weather the bad moments better." She had urgently sought God's guidance in the period when her health seemed to fail. A few years later, Eleanor could affirm, "Regardless of what happens, God is with me, and I am not going to be alone." This assurance came as a gift in the midst of a time of deep questioning and troubled health. It does not deny the realities of loss and pain she faces everyday. Her belief does not insulate her from ups and downs and fears—fears for her son and his family and for the future her grandchildren will face. Hope comes by acknowledging and facing the pain and the fears.

The God who gifted Eleanor with this assurance is in some ways more remote to her now than at earlier times in her life." I know less about God now than I did [as a young adult], but I experience God on a far deeper level." She admits that she struggles to find an image of God that feels adequate. "We all want to get hold of God and so we call God 'He,' but God is really the genesis of life." Eleanor resists imaging God as human. She has a powerfully evocative image for her relationship with God: that relationship is like a "watercolor painting where it just kind of oozes together and I finally give up my will and just merge with God." When she experienced that connection with grace, she found the hope for which she yearned. She describes those moments as "incredible peace." The God with whom Eleanor at times merges is a source of hope that sustains her and empowers her.

## REFLECTION

*Notice that hope does not deny the presence of hurt and brokenness. How have you experienced hope while addressing real brokenness in your life?*

Julia also testified eloquently to the gift of hope. Recall that she had experienced many losses and at times was near despair. The summer of drought seemed to echo and underline that difficult time. However, a weed with a deep taproot reminded her of God's life-giving presence and brought her out of the deep depression. That bit of green at the deepest place was grace. For Julia, God is like a taproot that sustains life. When she saw the small green at the end of the root, she experienced a return of hope.

Julia's God "is the ultimate Creator. I think the closest we come to the mind of God is the satisfaction in being creative." Julia hastens to assure us that she is not an artist, even though her words are filled with the complexity and depth of a fine work of art. She describes God in poetic terms: "I used to go to the beach and look at the rocks—how they were getting pounded and how they were washing up on one another and removing crags and smoothing. And [I realized] how that was happening in my life." The suffering she had experienced was a smoothing process she attributed to God. Julia knew that God could be trusted even when the smoothing was difficult.

She told us about the last week of her mother's life. At that time her Bible study group was reading the book of Job. She sat at her mother's bedside reading and thinking, *This is so parallel to what* is happening in her [Mom's] life and in my life and in my study. Her mother died. The next week, the theme of the Bible study was hope. Julia found echoes of her life in the story of Job and healing hope in the assurance of God's creative power. Hope did not deny the realities of brokenness and pain; it gave her strength to face them and to seek new life.

## REFLECTION

How do you see God as a creative force in your life and in the world? How do you experience the process of creation continuing?

The healing God for which Claude and others yearned came in the midst of crisis. Claude experienced a miracle and recovered from a life-threatening kidney disease. He felt a physical change during a time of prayer that he attributed to God's presence. He affirms, "Now I've experienced God so many times that it would be difficult for me not to have faith and know that there is somebody out there doing all of this." Glimpses of God's presence, care, and availability have left Claude with a deep hope. He believes that God saved his life for a purpose. Claude works diligently to discover what that purpose is.

Sophia went through a time of intense pain and alienation. She began to heal when she revealed her anger about this situation to a good friend. Discovering that sharing the pain and anger with her friend did not hurt their relationship eventually freed her to express anger toward God. She realized that she could be angry with God without risking the loss of God's love or acceptance. This assurance revived Sophia's hope. "It doesn't mean that everything is going to be good or easy or that there are not going to be hard times, but that life is still worth living and that the God who created us will travel with us on the journey."

Because she first discovered the freedom that acceptance brings through a friend, Sophia knows now that she experiences God through people. "We don't just find God in the sanctuary or on top of the cross. Many times I find God in people."

Sophia testifies that finding God was not automatic. "I do not think you can inherit your faith!" she exclaims. Sophia searched for God for much of her life. "I want everything to happen yesterday, but God's timetable is not the same as mine." This recognition has also reassured Sophia. "Now I understand that you can't merit God's love. It's given to you before you ask, and that's my security and my belief."

Her life now focuses on living in accepting relationships with God, herself, and others. In fact, this, to Sophia, is heaven: "to be comfortable with yourself, your neighbor, and God whom you know loves you, and to allow them to be who they are." With this comfort comes the recognition of deep differences, the need for the healing of relationships, and the effort needed to truly connect with another. Knowing of God's acceptance and love frees Sophia to accept and love herself and others. She knows the deep joy of living in relationship with God. Now she is free to hope.

## REFLECTION

*What are some ways you have found God's healing through the hands of another person? To whom do you look for God's presence?*

Some persons we interviewed had been deeply touched by suffering in war. Thomas, who as a young man witnessed the liberation of a Nazi death camp, finds his image of God in the faces of soldiers who are so like himself, "broken and sick, hurting and weak, with families and children, doing what they were asked to do for their country." All of his life he has seen God in the faces of those wounded by injustice. God enters into the experience of injustice. God shares, supports, and calls for new creation. Hope results from facing the injustices and the failures we inflict on one another. But more than that, hope inspires energy and work to make new lives and to seek justice. Thomas's profession as a lawyer and his volunteer work were responses to injustice. The hope that emerges from those pain-filled situations—situations of misery inflicted by other humans—does so because God is there. God is present in the faces of those who suffer. God suffers with them.

Monty's life and faith were also transformed by a war experience (in Vietnam). He saw drugs, inhumane treatment of civilians, insubordination, ineffective leaders, and even murder. When he returned home he tried to put his life back together. But, he says, "My west Texas faith was not enough to deal with what I saw." He was angry at the church's failure to deal with the realities of life. "I don't like the church. It didn't accept what was important to my life—my sexuality, my questions, my pain, and my hopes. If you're not accepting all of me, then I can't be wasting my time."

Yet, Monty continued to search for God. He enrolled in a spiritual formation program at a college, seeking to find God in the everyday moments of life and seeking to be a more faithful presence for God in his daily living. For Monty, God is in all of life, the extraordinary and the ordinary. He looks for that God with hope and confidence.

## REFLECTION

*Do you see God both in the ordinary and extraordinary circumstances of life? Talk with a friend about some of the ways you image God in the midst of life.*

War also radically impacted Franz's life. He was made part of the German army as a very young boy and under the subterfuge that he was going to school. Wounded, he ended up in the United States after a series of fortunate circumstances and with the help of his stepfather. Through this crisis, he carried theological notes, a Bible, and a confirmation certificate to remind him of God's presence. The question of God remained important even as the rest of his life settled down. He continued struggling to address his theological questions through logic and research. Franz now knows God as he searches for a logic to help him understand and make sense of events that sweep our lives up into history and sometimes leave us bereft of country and family.

His life of study has become satisfying and reassuring. "The Lord has tapped me on the shoulder," he says. The people of his congregation are the happy recipients of Franz's commitment to study as a search for God. They love to be in his classes. Indeed, God has tapped him on the shoulder and given him good work to do. Franz searches scripture to find evidence of God's plan. The study has yielded hope.

Like Franz, Bill has found hope through studying the Bible. He finds there an assurance of salvation and eternal life. "You may not have the plan, but [God] has the plan," he affirms. For Bill, God is salvation. He looks to God's promise of eternal life; it gives his life meaning and is the source of hope.

## REFLECTION

*What scriptures are a source of faith and hope for you? On which scriptures do you most often rely?*

Terri sees God as a present reality with whom she can be in relationship. When she had the insight that "God is like me," she began to pray to God in her bunk bed. This began a lifelong practice of conversing with God, sharing all the events, desires, and feelings of her life. She made a conscious decision to participate in that relationship and to make it primary in her life. She has never doubted that she can depend on God, the God who listens to her every need. From this close relationship she is gifted with hope.

Hilary affirms her hope by telling stories of God's care. For a time she lived in a house with no electricity or water. She had inherited the house but had no money. Bit by bit she worked her way out of that economic crisis. But she believes that God had a big hand in those events. "I know how God has worked for me. I can't say he'll do the same for you, but I'm saying it from what I feel and what I know he has done for me." She tells of one instance when she became critically ill with a strep infection that had spread to her blood. "I was lying in the hospital with tubes all over my body from my head to my toes, and they couldn't figure out what was wrong with me." After lying in intensive care for five days, Hilary called her cousin on the telephone, and they prayed together. "The next day I woke up, and it was amazing. It was like I had never been sick. I figured out what my problem was. I was too far away from the people who cared about me. It was just the Lord telling me, 'Hilary, you're going a bit too far. You're going out of your safety zone.'" She finds hope in the knowledge that "God has a plan for me. I never doubted that God was there."

## REFLECTION

*Do you use the language of "God's plan"? If so, when have you used this phrase to describe events in your life? If not, what do you think "God's plan" means?*

What enables some people to respond with resilience to suffering, fear, loss, and injustice while others despair? There is no simple answer to this question. No amount of effort can foist hope on another. Paradoxically, Christian hope is found in the recognition of the reality of brokenness. Jesus went to the cross because of betrayal, political conflict, and hatred. In spite of this, the proclamation of the Christian story is that the same God who created also stood beside the Hebrew people as they were buffeted by political forces, offered the vision of hope to the whole world through Isaiah's vision (Isa. 65:17-25), and concretely offered new life through the life of Jesus, the Incarnate One. Since God did not desert Christ or the world in death, God is the source of the Resurrection and the resurrections we are offered in our lives. That same God is working, as Paul so eloquently describes in Romans 8:18-25, through the groaning of creation to give birth to the children of God and to their hope.

Hope is complex. For hope to be real, evil and brokenness

must be recognized as well as the gracious presence of a God who offers new life, heals, opens options, and supports. Denial of evil, insulating oneself behind protective walls, attempting to secure and control the future, and falling into despair—all of these responses deny the new life that is present in God's continual process of creation.

## REFLECTION

*What persons do you know who respond with resilience to issues of suffering, fear, loss, and injustice? What enables their resilience? How do you respond to suffering, fear, loss, and injustice—with hope or despair?*

Many holiday greetings during December 2001 focused on the events of September 11, honoring the gifts friends bring to life, expressing confusion, reaching out to family members, and offering blessings. That December, friends sent us a thoughtful Christmas letter. They, like others, were looking for something to say in response to the hurt, confusion, and pain. Their letter read:

Working on an assignment, our granddaughter, a college freshman, called to ask us two simple questions:

1. What is the good life?
2. How did you find out?

Her call came in the midst of a year when we could not believe all we had seen and heard—people jumping to their deaths while others, in uniform, climbed to their deaths, hoping to save a life or two before sacrificing their own. In was a year when we heard pundits thinking the unthinkable out loud, fashioning a rationale for torture and building a sane case for violence in response to violence. And it also was a year in which we saw pain and suffering, not only on the faces of strangers on television, but on the faces of those we love the most.

So how do we talk about "the good life" without being callow or callous or cynical? And without being overwhelmed by "heaviness of spirit"? And without, on the other hand, being depressingly chirpy and chipper?

In the end, I surprised myself by being more religious than I expected to be. The question about "the good life" is a good Greek question, but it requires for me a Judeo-Christian answer. We are not clueless. His name is Jesus. In our kind of a world, Dietrich Bonhoeffer said during World War II, "only a suffering God can help." Since September 11, we have all felt more vulnerable, but that's the way we were supposed to be all along—with exposed nerves, wise and tragic hearts, pierced hands and an indomitable spirit.

The message of Christmas—and the answer to the question "What is the good life?"—is that we are not alone. Emmanuel, the suffering God, is with us and ours and will be to the end of our days—in joy and in sorrow, in sickness and in health, in war and peace. In times of prosperity, we pray, may God-with-us fill our hearts with thanksgiving and in the day of trouble, may our trust in him not fail.[2]

What a powerful expression of the reality of hope grounded in the events of life, respecting both the loss and gift present in life and reaching out to the hope that stands by and calls forward. These kinds of theological meanings are present among the people of God as they seek to understand a creating, redeeming, and sustaining power in their midst.

## REFLECTION

*Think about those two questions that the granddaughter asked: (1) For you, what is the good life? (2) How did you find out?*

# The Welcome Table

The words of the spiritual, written during the time of slavery, need to be repeated often today:

> I'm going to sit at the welcome table
> Shout my troubles over
> Walk and talk with Jesus
> Tell God how you treat me
> One of these days!

The welcome table is exactly what we found as we invited these faithful persons into conversation about their lives. We heard stories of loss, betrayal, abuse, injustice, despair, and hurt. But we also heard stories of new life, grace, meaningful vocation, acceptance, and hope.

Almost every interview ended with the words *thank you*. We thanked these persons for inviting us onto the holy grounds of their lives. They thanked us because they found a time and a place to question, to reflect, and to express how they are seeking to connect faith to life. They prayed aloud that the openness they had experienced in the interviews to questions about their lives and faith traditions would be accepted in their churches, congregations that they loved. Indeed, they wanted to sit at a welcome table.

Moreover, they yearned for opportunities to "tell their troubles over"—to express the details of living but not in a narcissistic, pride-filled way. They wanted to walk and talk with Jesus. In other words, they sought to understand how their faith connected to living, making life meaningful and empowering it with grace, vocation, and hope. The answers they gave are not always consistent. Often they push boundaries. Sometimes they are even misdirected. But they represent a yearning to know the God whose grace-filled presence is found in life. And these persons yearn to be God's agents of faith and hope by building communities of meaning, justice, healing, and new creation.

These yearnings are deeply embedded in our lives from the time of creation. At times we misuse our gifts and hurt others, but we can build foundations for faithful living by remaining open to God, listening deeply to others and to the presence of God in their lives, attempting to understand ways we cause pain, and asking for forgiveness as we work to make situations right.

The church is a community that offers a place, a tradition, and practices of attending that could assist us as we "tell our troubles over, walk and talk with Jesus," and seek to be faithful.

May we pray that the church indeed can become a welcome table, open to difference and questioning.

May we pray that faith traditions can continue to be open to the enlivening presence of God.

May we pray that common work for new creation can result from listening to those who are different from us and who hold differing religious commitments.

May we continue to yearn for God.

By seeking God in the midst of life, we open ourselves to the groaning of the creation, to the birth of the children of God.

# GROUP DISCUSSION GUIDE

by Tracey L. Henderson

Yearning is a natural part of our human condition. Many Christians have felt or will someday feel a yearning for God. This study is designed to help you explore your yearnings as you live out your faith in your daily life. The goal of the discussion guide is to provide a framework through which small groups of faithful people can share their stories on a deep level, relating life experiences to their beliefs about God and Jesus Christ.

Although designed for small groups, this discussion guide is equally appropriate for couples. Reading and discussing *Yearning for God* together can be a tremendously enriching experience for Christian couples. This guide can serve as a launch point to help couples learn to communicate with each other about their faith.

## Practical Suggestions for Leaders

### Your Role

As a group or session leader, your most important role is to facilitate meaningful participation and sharing among all group members.

Your job is not to teach but to listen and encourage. Use this study guide as a starting point, but be flexible enough to follow the Holy Spirit's leading and accommodate the group's interests.

## Setting Ground Rules

If your group does not already have a covenant, the introductory session provides an opportunity for participants to develop a set of ground rules. Make sure that confidentiality, punctuality, nonjudgmental listening, and freedom to "pass" (not answer certain questions) are included.

## Planning the Sessions

Each session follows the same pattern, within which you have flexibility to accommodate different meeting lengths, group preferences, and learning styles. Most headings within each session contain a number of bulleted options. Under each heading, choose the options that will most likely interest your group and that best fit your time constraints. Bulleted options are for group discussion unless otherwise noted. The study guide for each session is addressed to all participants. Instructions specifically for session leaders appear in bracketed italics.

## Prayer

Each session begins and ends with prayer. You may choose to pray extemporaneously or read a written prayer that you select or write ahead of time. As session leader, you may lead the prayers yourself or rotate this responsibility in the group. Each session also includes a time for sharing prayer concerns and praying together. Use whatever method is most comfortable for the group. If participants are not yet accustomed to group prayer, you may want to start with silent prayer in the first session (opened and closed by the session leader) and progress through a series of different prayer techniques during the study.

## Question Box

Often in a group setting, people have ideas, opinions, hopes, fears, or questions they long to express, but they may not feel comfortable doing so verbally. Writing down these thoughts anonymously and placing them in a "question box" for group discussion creates a safe space for expression and helps build trust for deeper communication within the group. To make a question box, cut a slot in the top of a shoe box and decorate the box and lid. Place slips of paper and pens beside the box. Each session provides an opportunity to use the question box, but no one should feel obligated to use it.

## Journals

Encourage everyone to write their reactions, questions, and comments in a journal as they do their weekly reading. Each session provides an opportunity for personal reflection and journal writing, so participants should bring their journals to each group meeting. All sessions close with a key question for participants to think about during the coming week. Ask everyone to write his or her responses in their journals and be ready to discuss them at the beginning of the next session.

## Materials

Bring the following materials to the first session. Keep the materials (except for Bibles, study books, and journals) in a box to bring with you to all subsequent sessions.

- Bible (each participant should bring a Bible)
- copies of this book (one per participant)
- notebooks (one per participant, to be used as journals)
- songbooks or hymnals
- question box
- blank slips of paper
- pencils or pens
- 1 die (from a set of dice)

- 4 by 6 cards (one per participant, to be used as prayer cards)
- 1 sheet of poster board
- felt-tip marker
- envelopes

## Introductory Session

This session is recommended for all groups, especially for new groups or situations in which group members do not already know one another well. [Leader: If your group chooses not to start with this introductory session, please include the following two activities in Session 1. You will refer to these activities again in the closing session.]

### Approaching Holy Ground

Open with prayer, inviting God's presence in the group and asking for God's guidance throughout this study.

### Building Community

Greet one another. One by one, introduce yourselves and tell one fact about yourself that no one else in the room is likely to know. Have everyone roll a die and answer one of the following questions according to the number rolled. [Leader: You may want to write these questions on the board.]

1. What is your earliest memory of church?

2. What book have you read that was especially meaningful to you?

3. What is your favorite hymn? Why?

4. What movie or TV program do you think presents some good, positive values?

5. If you could spend half an hour with anyone in the

world that you've never met, whom would you choose? What would you ask him or her?

6. If someone gave you $10,000 to donate to a charitable cause, where would you send the money? Why?

Tell what you look forward to in this study and what you hope to gain.

## Embarking on the Study

[Distribute a book and a blank journal to each participant. Explain the weekly format and time frame of group meetings. If the group chooses to rotate responsibilities such as session leadership, hospitality, or leading opening and closing prayers, set up the schedule for the following ten weeks. Place the question box in a convenient location and explain its purpose.]

Often people have concerns as they embark on a new small-group experience. As individuals, write down on slips of paper any questions, concerns, or apprehensions you might have about the experience you are about to begin together. Do not sign your name. Place the papers in the question box. When everyone has finished, read and discuss the list of concerns. As a group, what can you do to alleviate these concerns?

What ground rules does your group need to ensure trust and open communication? As a group, develop a list of guidelines that everyone can agree on. Consider these ground rules as promises you make to one another for the duration of your time together. [Write the list on a piece of poster board and display it at each session.]

## Focusing on Scripture

Listen as someone reads Psalm 42:1-2. If you know the song "As the Deer" by Martin Nystrom, based on Psalm 42, sing it together. Then close your eyes and listen as the passage is read again. As you listen, imagine you are the psalm writer. Pay attention to your feelings.

• What thoughts or feelings did this Bible passage evoke in you?

- Could you easily identify with the author of Psalm 42? Have you ever felt such a strong longing for God? If so, what prompted it? To what degree has your longing been satisfied?

- If you have never felt such a longing for God, what have you longed for?

[If you skip the introductory session, please do the following activity in Session 1.]

[Distribute paper, a pen, and an envelope to each person.]

Individually, spend time silently reflecting on this question: "What do you truly yearn for in your life right now?" When you are finished, write your response on a piece of paper, place it in an envelope, seal the envelope, write your name on it, and give it to the session leader. Do not discuss responses in the group. You will open your envelope again in the last session.

[Collect the envelopes; keep them in the supply box until the last session.]

## Practicing Theological Reflection

[If you skip the introductory session, please do the following activity in Session 1.]

As individuals, spend a few minutes thinking about the following questions, and write your thoughts in your journal. Then share your responses with the group.

- What comes to mind when you hear the word theology?

- What persons do you think of as "theologians"? What do they do? What qualifies them to do it?

- What, if anything, prevents you from thinking or living theologically?

## Encouraging One Another

Go around the room, giving each person an opportunity to briefly talk about a concern for which he or she would appreciate prayer support. (Everyone should feel free to pass.)

As a group, spend some time in prayer for one another.

[Distribute 4 by 6 cards and ask everyone to write his or her name at the top of one side. Then collect the cards, shuffle them, and have everyone draw a card. If anyone draws his or her own name, have that person swap cards with someone else.]

Over the coming week, pray daily for the person named on your card. On the prayer card, jot today's date and a note to remind you of any special prayer concerns this person mentioned.

Place the card in your Bible or study book and bring it with you to the next session. (Each week, cards will be reshuffled and everyone will draw a different name.)

## Looking Forward

- Over the next week, read chapter 1, "Life-Shaped Faith: Theology in Everyday Life."

- Over the coming week, pay attention to anything that causes you to think about God even for a moment. In your journal, write each "theological prompt" you observed. Was it an object, an event in your life, a conversation, a feeling?

## Going Forth

Close with prayer, thanking God for this time of Christian community and praying that God will help us be more alert to God's presence in our lives over the coming week.

# SESSION 1

## LIFE-SHAPED FAITH: THEOLOGY IN EVERYDAY LIFE

### Approaching Holy Ground

Open with prayer, inviting God's presence and guidance during this group meeting.

### Building Community

In pairs, take a few minutes to discuss the following questions:

- In a typical week, how much time do you spend talking about spiritual matters such as God, your faith, the meaning of life, and so forth?

- How do your answers compare to the amount of time you spend on other activities (for example, doing chores, watching television, etc.)?

- The authors identified the persons they interviewed as "faithful people." What does it mean to be a faithful person? Describe someone you consider faithful.

- Last week, you were asked to pay attention to the events or conditions that prompted you to think about God. Talk about your experiences. Do any common themes emerge?

- [Hand out blank slips of paper and pencils.] If you have questions, comments, or issues related to chapter 1 that you wish to discuss in the group, write them down and place them in the question box.

## Focusing on Scripture

Listen as someone reads aloud Luke 24:13-35. As you listen, think about the setting and why Jesus might have chosen this moment to appear to the two disciples.

- What stood out most for you about this story?

- Why do you think Jesus chose this moment to appear to the two disciples?

How can talking about our faith in the context of the events of our daily lives open us to experiencing God's presence?

When have you felt the presence of God while sharing your beliefs, feelings, questions, or struggles with another person? What insights did you gain through this experience?

[If you did not have an introductory session, do the envelope activity now. (See the Focusing on Scripture section of the introductory session.) You will refer back to this activity in the closing session.]

## Practicing Theological Reflection

- The persons interviewed for this book shared a common theme: hunger for meaning. When have you experienced a hunger for meaning? Describe what you felt at the time.

- Frederick seemed uncomfortable discussing certain aspects of his faith for fear of sounding "a little overboard on religion." How comfortable do you feel talking about your faith? With whom do you talk about it? What holds you back? Which aspects of your faith do you find easiest to talk about? Which are the most difficult? Why?

- [If you did not do the introductory session, do the activity in the Practicing Theological Reflection section of the introductory session now. You will refer back to this activity in the closing session.]

- Read the quotation from Educating Christians, page 21 of this book. What does it say about theology? Now turn to your journal and reread what you wrote about your understanding of theology. How do these two views compare?

- How did Frederick's experience of caring for his wife lead him to engage in theological reflection? What meaning was he able to draw from this experience? If you were in Frederick's position, would you make the same choices? How does your answer relate to your own faith and convictions?

- [Open the question box and read any questions or thoughts that were submitted.] As a group, discuss any issues that have not already been addressed.

- The authors described eight types of spiritual yearning expressed by the people they interviewed. Going around the room, take turns reading the brief explanation of one type of yearning until all have been read. As individuals, spend some time in silent reflection. With which type of yearning do you identify most closely? Why? Write down your responses in your journal. (Do not discuss your conclusions as a group.)

## Encouraging One Another

- Share prayer concerns with the group as you feel comfortable.

- As a group, pray with and for one another.

- [Collect the prayer cards, reshuffle them, and have everyone draw a new card.] In the coming week, pray daily for the person named on your card. Write on the card special prayer concerns of this person. Remember to bring the card with you to the next session.

## Looking Forward

- Read chapter 2, "Yearning for Vocation," for next week.

- Over the coming week, reflect on the work you do (including unpaid work). Do you view your work primarily as a vocation or a way to make a living? How closely do your faith and work connect? Write your reflections in your journal.

## Going Forth

Close with prayer, thanking God for this time of community and asking for clear guidance on God's will for your life and work.

# SESSION 2

## YEARNING FOR VOCATION

### Approaching Holy Ground

Open with prayer, inviting God's presence and guidance.

### Building Community

- If you could choose any method by which God would send you an unmistakably clear message about God's will for your life and work, what would it be?

- Over the past week, you were asked to reflect on the work you do (including unpaid work) and how closely your work connects with your faith. Discuss your insights. Do any common themes emerge?

- Write any questions, comments, or issues related to the reading that you wish to discuss, and place them in the question box.

### Focusing on Scripture

Listen as someone reads aloud 1 Kings 19:1-18. While you listen, imagine yourself in Elijah's position. What are you thinking and feeling? Listen to verses 3-5 again.

- What kind of response from God do you think Elijah hoped for?

- When have you felt like Elijah? What brought you to that place?

- What parallels can you draw between Elijah's experience and Eleanor's story as described in the reading?

## Practicing Theological Reflection

- How do a job and a vocation differ? What do you consider your vocation? How did you come to view it as such?

- Eleanor described a time in college when a professor rattled her faith. Have you ever had anyone challenge or shake up your faith? What was the result?

- Has your life ever taken a huge turn without your intending it? How did it happen? Looking back, how do you see God in connection with this change?

- When have you experienced a lack of direction? How did it make you feel? What did you do about it? In what ways did your faith provide comfort or guidance?

- Eleanor yearned to know whether God approved of her life. As individuals, reflect on the following question: "What do you think it takes to gain God's approval?" Write your response in your journal. If you wish, share your thoughts with the group.

- [Open the question box and read any questions or thoughts that were submitted.] As a group, discuss any issues that have not already been addressed.

## Encouraging One Another

- Share prayer concerns with the group as you feel comfortable.

- As a group, pray with and for one another.

- [Collect the prayer cards, reshuffle them, and have everyone draw a new card.] Over the coming week, pray daily for the person named on your card. Write on the card any special prayer concerns of this person. Remember to bring the card to the next session.

## Looking Forward

- Before next week's meeting, read chapter 3, "Yearning for Grace." As you read, note your reactions in your journal along with any questions or issues from the reading that you wish to discuss with the group.

- Over the coming week, reflect on what grace means to you and ways you have experienced God's grace in your life. Write your reflections in your journal.

## Going Forth

Close with prayer, thanking God for this time of community and asking for clear assurance of God's presence in your life over the coming week.

# SESSION 3

## YEARNING FOR GRACE

## Approaching Holy Ground

Open with prayer, inviting God's presence and guidance during this group meeting.

## Building Community

- Sing "Amazing Grace" together. Talk about any special meaning this hymn may have for you.

- Over the past week, you were asked to reflect on God's grace. What does grace mean to you?

• Write any questions, comments, or issues related to the reading that you wish to discuss, and place them in the question box.

## Focusing on Scripture

Take a few moments of silence to think about your own concept of God's grace. Then listen as three people read the following Bible passages: John 3:16; John 15:9-15; and Romans 8:35-39. As you listen, think about how these passages relate to your concept of grace.

• What do these Bible passages tell you about God's grace?

• [Leader: Ask everyone to close his/her eyes as you read aloud all three passages again, pausing after each one.] What image does each passage bring to mind for you? How do these images illustrate God's grace? Take a few minutes to sketch these images or write your reflections in your journal. If you are comfortable doing so, share your insights with the group.

## Practicing Theological Reflection

• What image would you choose to describe the connection God desires with humans? What kind of connection would you like to have with God?

• How could the question "Whose am I?" instead of "Who am I?" help you focus more on God's grace and less on your own accomplishments? In your journal, write a brief introduction to yourself based on your identity as a child of God. In pairs, exchange these introductions. How does this introduction differ from the way you would introduce yourself at a professional or social event? Why might these two images differ?

• Describe a time in your life when God seemed especially near. What was happening? What made you aware of God's presence?

• Julia and Wilma both described experiences of God's grace during times of great despair and loss. Recall a time when you felt really low or overwhelmed. What lifted you out of the depth? Was there a sign that you attribute to God?

- Julia, Lan, and Terri related childhood experiences of God's grace. In what ways did you experience God's presence as a child? How did those early experiences shape your faith today?

- How do you reconcile the concept of God's grace with the fact that "bad things do happen to God's people"?

- Did the tragedy of September 11 change the way you live? The way you approach your faith? Explain. Have these changes endured in the time since the tragedy?

- How did the church help you cope with the 9/11 tragedies? What could the church have done better in this regard?

- [Open the question box and read any questions or thoughts that were submitted.] As a group, discuss any issues that have not already been addressed.

## Encouraging One Another

- Share prayer concerns with the group as you feel comfortable.

- As a group, pray with and for one another.

- [Collect the prayer cards, reshuffle them, and have everyone draw a new card.] Over the coming week, pray daily for the person named on your card. Write on the card any special prayer concerns of this person. Bring the card with you to the next session.

## Looking Forward

- Before next week's meeting, read chapter 4, "Yearning for Meaning and Healing." As you read, note your reactions in your journal along with any questions or issues from the reading that you wish to discuss with the group.

- Over the coming week, reflect on times of crisis or loss you have experienced. When did you feel that Jesus walked with you in your suffering? When did you feel that God was out of reach? What meaning can you make from these times of trial?

Write your reflections in your journal.

## Going Forth

Close with prayer, thanking God for this time of community and asking for God's strength and comfort over the coming week as you reflect on times of trial in your life.

# SESSION 4

## YEARNING FOR MEANING AND HEALING

## Approaching Holy Ground

Open with prayer, inviting God's presence, guidance, and comfort during this group meeting.

## Building Community

- Are you able to find comfort in scripture when you are discouraged or facing a crisis? If so, which Bible passages do you find most comforting?

- Write any questions, comments, or issues related to the reading that you wish to discuss, and place them in the question box.

## Focusing on Scripture

Think of a time when you felt discouraged. With this situation in mind, listen as someone reads 2 Corinthians 1:3-7 and Romans 8:26-27. As you listen, think about the images these passages bring to your mind and about how you feel as you hear these passages.

- What does this passage from 2 Corinthians say about suffering and comfort?

- What images did these two passages bring to mind for you? How did hearing them make you feel?

- In what ways have your own experiences of trial or suffering helped you comfort someone else?

## Practicing Theological Reflection

- What is the first experience of loss you can remember? How did you understand God's activity in the situation?

- Respond to the quotation, "Personal crisis is often a powerful catalyst for spiritual growth." How have you found this true in your own experience?

- Can you think of a time when going through a struggle made you stronger or, in Monty's words, was "the best thing that ever happened" to you? If so, tell your story.

- How do you make sense of suffering? Discuss the following contrasting explanations of suffering. Which do you find most likely? most comforting? Why?

  - God works out everything, including our suffering, for the ultimate good. Therefore, all suffering has a purpose and is part of God's will.

  - Suffering is a result of sin. We bring suffering on ourselves through sin.

  - Another explanation you've heard for suffering.

- Reflect silently on these questions: When have you been really angry with God? What did you learn about God from this experience? Write your responses in your journal. If you wish, share your responses with the group.

- Have you, like Claude, ever experienced what you believed to be a call from God, only to find the door slammed in your face? If so, what happened? How did you feel? What meaning were you able to find in the situation?

- Have you ever felt as though God was testing you? If so, how? Do you feel you passed the test? What, if anything, did you gain from the experience?

- Do you believe God performs miraculous healing now? Why or why not? Why do you think some people are healed of their illnesses and others are not? Where is God in each of these outcomes?

- When have you experienced God's protection or healing? What was it like? With whom did you discuss this experience? How did that person (those persons) receive your story? Did you talk about this experience at your church? Why or why not?

- When have you felt surrounded and comforted by your faith community? What did that experience teach you about God?

- [Open the question box and read any questions or thoughts that were submitted.] As a group, discuss any issues that have not already been addressed.

## Encouraging One Another

- Share prayer concerns with the group as you feel comfortable.

- As a group, pray with and for one another.

- [Collect the prayer cards, reshuffle them, and have everyone draw a new card.] Over the coming week, pray daily for the person named on your card. Write on the card special prayer concerns of this person. Bring the card with you to the next session.

## Looking Forward

- Before next week's meeting, read chapter 5, "Yearning for Justice." As you read, note your reactions in your journal along with any questions or issues from the reading that you wish to discuss with the group.

- Over the coming week, reflect on what the world would be like if God's justice were a reality for all people. Write a description or draw a sketch of this "just world" in your journal.

## Going Forth

Pray, thanking God for this time of community and asking God to show you clearly your own special role in working toward justice for all God's people.

# SESSION 5

## YEARNING FOR JUSTICE

## Approaching Holy Ground

Open with prayer, inviting God's presence and guidance.

## Building Community

- Over the past week, you were asked to imagine what the world would be like if God's justice were a reality for all people. Describe your vision or show your drawing of a truly just world to the group.

- If you could ask God any "why" question (and receive a clear answer), what would it be?

- When have you witnessed injustice against another person or group? How did it make you feel? What, if anything, did you do about it at the time?

- Write down any questions, comments, or issues related to the reading, and place them in the question box.

## Focusing on Scripture

Have someone read Micah 6:6-8 aloud. As you listen, think about what these passages mean in the context of today's culture.

- In your journal rewrite the passage in your own words as it applies to your life today. Share your results with the group.

- As a group, discuss any differences you see between what the Bible teaches about justice, what is said about justice in church, and what you actually do about justice in practice.

- How do we "seek justice" in every facet of life? Which justice issues are closest to your heart?

## Practicing Theological Reflection

- When have you personally encountered an adversary, only to discover that your enemy was as human as you are? How did this revelation of common humanity change your relationship with this person?

- What is the difference between justice and retribution? Recall a time when you were personally wronged. How did you respond? In your response, did you seek justice or retribution?

- Do you think the U.S. response to the tragedy of September 11 represented justice or retribution? Do you agree with this response? Why or why not?

- Thomas viewed the silence of the church in the face of the Holocaust as "a monumental failure of Christianity." How do you think the church should have responded to the horror of the Holocaust? Can you think of any current situations in which the church closes its eyes to injustice? If so, what? How do you think the church should respond? How could you personally respond?

How could you influence the church's response?

- Franz asserted that he had attended church for the wrong reasons—he wanted "something out of it." What is the most important role of the church for you? Do you think it is right or wrong to want to "get something out of" church? Explain. What, if anything, do you want or expect from your church? How well does it meet your needs?

- How do you respond to Thomas's conviction that justice is up to us? What do you feel called to do (that you are not already doing) in pursuit of justice for all God's people?

- [Open the question box and read any questions or thoughts that were submitted.] As a group, discuss any issues that have not already been addressed.

## Encouraging One Another

- Share prayer concerns with the group as you feel comfortable.

- As a group, pray with and for one another.

- [Collect the prayer cards, reshuffle them, and have everyone draw a new card.] Over the coming week, pray daily for the person named on your card. Write on the card special prayer concerns of this person. Remember to bring the card with you to the next session.

## Looking Forward

- Before next week's meeting, read chapter 6, "Yearning for Assurance." As you read, note your reactions in your journal along with any questions or issues from the reading you wish to discuss with the group.

- Over the coming week, reflect on the assurances that your faith provides. In what matters of faith do you feel complete assurance? What kind of assurances do you still seek? Write your reflections in your journal.

## Going Forth

Pray, thanking God for this time of community. Ask for assurance over the coming week of God's unfailing love for all group members.

# SESSION 6

## YEARNING FOR ASSURANCE

## Approaching Holy Ground

Open with prayer, inviting God's presence and guidance during this group meeting.

## Building Community

- Sing together the hymn "Blessed Assurance" by Fanny Crosby. When have you experienced a sense of blessed assurance? What did it feel like? Has this sense of assurance stayed with you ever since, or does it come and go?

- Talk about your reflections on assurance over the past week. In what matters of faith do you feel assurance? What kinds of assurances are you still looking for?

- When you need assurance, what Bible passages do you find helpful? Look up several of these passages and take turns reading them aloud. Why do you find these passages reassuring?

- Write any questions, comments, or issues related to the reading that you wish to discuss, and place them in the question box.

## Focusing on Scripture

Close your eyes and listen as someone reads Psalm 121 aloud. Let the words of this psalm wash over you, and pay attention to your feelings as you hear them. Then, in silence, take a few minutes to reflect on the following questions and write your responses in your journal. When done, share your reflections with the group.

- What feelings does this psalm evoke in you?
- What kind of assurance does it offer you?

## Practicing Theological Reflection

- The people interviewed in chapter 6 talked about different aspects of assurance. As individuals, silently reflect on whether you already feel complete assurance or you are still seeking assurance for the faith issues listed below. Be totally honest with yourself. Then discuss your responses as a group. For which of these faith issues is assurance most important to you? On what other faith questions do you yearn for assurance?

  - Assurance that God loves you and cares about what happens to you.

  - Assurance that you are going to heaven.

  - Assurance that God approves of your life.

  - Assurance that your faith "makes sense" and is consistent with other facets of your life, experience, and knowledge.

- Have you made a decision for Christian discipleship? If so, did you do so at a specific time, or was it a gradual process? How did you come to your decision? Who helped or influenced you? If you have not made that decision, what issues do you need resolved? What kind of assurances do you need to feel certain that you want to follow Jesus?

- In matters of faith, are you more of a "head" person or a "heart" person? Do you seek to have your faith make rational sense in the context of your life experiences? Or do you find comfort when your faith just "feels right"? What does your answer tell you about yourself?

- Wilma spoke of her struggle to accept "the mystery" of God. Describe your comfort level with ambiguity and unanswered questions about God. Do you think that after we die God will answer all our questions, or will mysteries remain?

- When has someone given you an easy, pat answer as you struggled with a deep, complex spiritual question? How did you react? Did the simplicity of the answer comfort or frustrate you?

- [Open the question box and read any questions or thoughts that were submitted.] As a group, discuss any issues that have not already been addressed.

## Encouraging One Another
- Share prayer concerns with the group as you feel comfortable.

- As a group, pray with and for one another.

- [Collect the prayer cards, reshuffle them, and have everyone draw a new card.] Over the coming week, pray daily for the person named on your card. Write on the card any special prayer concerns of this person. Bring the card with you to the next session.

## Looking Forward
- Before next week's meeting, read chapter 7, "Yearning to Be Known and Accepted." As you read, note your reactions in your journal along with any questions or issues from the reading that you wish to discuss with the group.

- Over the coming week, reflect on times you felt known and accepted and on times you felt excluded or rejected. Where was God in these situations? Write reflections in your journal.

## Going Forth
Read Psalm 23 together. Spend a minute in silent reflection and thankfulness for the assurance that God will always be with us.

Close with prayer, thanking God for this time together and asking God to show you ways to help welcome and accept people who may feel excluded from your faith community.

# SESSION 7

## YEARNING TO BE KNOWN AND ACCEPTED

### Approaching Holy Ground
Open with prayer, inviting God's presence and guidance during this group meeting.

### Building Community
- Tell about a situation in which you felt both known and accepted. Who knew and accepted you? How did it make you feel?

- In pairs, tell about a time when you felt excluded in church or another group setting. Why do you think you were excluded? How did it make you feel? How did you respond?

- Write any questions, comments, or issues related to the reading that you wish to discuss, and place them in the question box.

### Focusing on Scripture
Close your eyes and listen as someone reads Psalm 139:1-18 and 23-24 aloud. As you listen, intentionally rest in God's presence.

- Do you believe, as the psalmist suggests, that God knows everything about you, including all your thoughts and motivations? Why or why not?

• Read Galatians 3:26-29 and Romans 15:1-7. What do these scriptures tell you about being accepted and accepting others?

• What do these passages say about acceptance in the church? What do you think Paul meant when he wrote them? How do you think your church can apply these passages today? Be specific.

• In your opinion, do Christians have to agree on everything in order to be "unified"? Justify your position. Do you think there are any issues about which all Christians must agree? If so, what are they?

## Practicing Theological Reflection

• In silence, take a few minutes to reflect individually on the following questions. Write your thoughts in your journal.

  – How well do you feel other people in your faith community really know you? How well do you think others in your church would accept you if they knew everything about you?

  – What aspects of yourself do you hesitate to reveal to others at church? Do you believe that your church might not welcome parts of you?

  If you feel comfortable, share your reflections.

• Sophia's church was divided over the controversial issue of racial integration. What issues in your church divide people? Are people able to discuss these tensions openly, or are these issues "taboo"? What topics are too controversial to raise in your church? What do you think would happen if they were discussed openly? Do you think these issues should be raised? Why or why not? If you said yes, what could you do to help the church provide constructive opportunities to raise them?

• Have you ever taken a stand for accepting others? What happened?

How was your position received?

- Who is not present at your church's table? Who is not present in your study group? Have they been excluded intentionally, or is their absence due to other factors? Explain. What can you do to actively welcome those who are not present?

- *[Open the question box and read any questions or thoughts that were submitted.]* As a group, discuss any issues that have not already been addressed.

## Encouraging One Another

- Share prayer concerns with the group as you feel comfortable.

- As a group, pray with and for one another.

- *[Collect the prayer cards, reshuffle them, and have everyone draw a new card.]* Over the next week, pray daily for the person named on your card. Write on the card any special prayer concerns of this person. Remember to bring the card with you to the next session.

## Looking Forward

- Before next week's meeting, read chapter 8, "Yearning for the New Creation." As you read, note your reactions in your journal along with any questions or issues from the reading that you wish to discuss with the group.

- Over the coming week, reflect on what you have learned about God or your faith from people who are different from you. Write your reflections in your journal.

## Going Forth

Close with a prayer of thanksgiving for God's unconditional love and acceptance.

# SESSION 8

## YEARNING FOR
## THE NEW CREATION

*[You will need the following additional materials for this session: plain paper (for drawing or painting), markers, colored pencils, watercolor paints and paintbrushes, small paper cups and water.]*

## Approaching Holy Ground

Open with prayer, inviting God's presence and guidance during this group meeting.

## Building Community

- Tell about a time when you learned an important lesson from someone who was different from you or from whom you did not expect to learn anything. How have you applied this lesson in your own life?

- Have you ever lived in or traveled to a different culture? If so, what did you learn about yourself from this experience? What did you learn about your faith? How did the experience change you? If not, imagine that you had an opportunity to serve on a short-term mission trip for a few weeks in any culture of your choice. Where would you go, and what would you do? Explain your choices. What do you think you might gain from the experience?

- Write any questions, comments, or issues related to the reading that you wish to discuss, and place them in the question box.

## Focusing on Scripture

Close your eyes and listen as someone reads Revelation 21:3-4. Spend time in silence, imagining what the new creation will be like.

• Using watercolor paints, markers, or colored pencils, create a picture that depicts your image of the new creation. (Don't worry about being artistic.) As a variation, you may choose to write poetry or prose describing this image. When you finish, share and explain your depiction of the new creation. What common themes do you see? How do these images inspire you?

• Now read Isaiah 65:17-25 as a group by going around the room and having each person read a verse in turn. Again, pay attention to the images this passage brings to your mind. How does the prophet Isaiah's depiction of a new heaven and a new earth compare with your own images of the new creation?

• When and where do you think the new creation will become a reality? When we die and go to heaven? When Jesus comes again to earth? When the people of God join together to eradicate hunger, poverty, and violence from the world? At some other time and place? Do you think you will ever experience the new creation?

## Practicing Theological Reflection

• When have you caught a glimpse of the new creation promised in the Bible? Describe the experience.

• What positive insights might other religions or faith traditions offer Christianity? When have you gained understanding from a source completely outside of traditional Christianity that helped you make sense of your faith?

• Can you imagine any situations where encounters with other religions might harm Christians or undermine the Christian faith? Explain. How can we find balance between the benefits and any potential risks of interfaith encounters?

- How do you reconcile the need to accept differences and respect other people's cultures and religious traditions with Jesus' command to "go . . . and make disciples of all nations" (Matt. 28:19)?

- When have you experienced a group setting where you could love one other and accept your differences? How did this feel? What made it possible for this loving acceptance to happen?

- When have you been unable to overcome or move beyond differences? What was the result?

- What does community mean to you? How can you create or achieve community? After discussing these questions as a group, read Acts 2:43-47. Do your descriptions of community resemble the description of the fellowship of believers assembled at Pentecost? Do you think the type of community described in this passage is realistic today? Why or why not? Would you want to participate fully in this type of community? What would you have to give up to do so? What would you gain? Do you see any similarities between the community described in Acts 2:43-47 and your vision of the new creation? Explain.

- How do you think God calls you to help bring about the new creation?

- [Open the question box and read any questions or thoughts.] As a group, discuss any issues that have not already been addressed.

## Encouraging One Another

- Share prayer concerns with the group as you feel comfortable.

- As a group, pray with and for one another.

- [Collect the prayer cards, reshuffle them, and have everyone draw a new card.] Over the next week, pray daily for the person named on your card. Write on the card special prayer concerns of this person. Bring the card with you to the next session.

## Looking Forward

- Before next week's meeting, read chapter 9, "Yearning for Hope, Yearning for God." As you read, note your reactions in your journal along with any questions or issues from the reading that you wish to discuss with the group.

- Over the coming week, pay attention to your images of God. What name do you call God when you pray? How do you envision God? How do you view your relationship with God? Write your reflections in your journal.

## Going Forth

Close with a prayer of thanksgiving for this time of community, and ask God to bring hope to a troubled world yearning for God's new creation.

---

# SESSION 9

## YEARNING FOR HOPE, YEARNING FOR GOD

*[Additional materials required for this session include a large sheet of paper and tape for posting it. If possible, find a copy of the children's book In God's Name by Sandy Eisenberg Sasso and bring it with you to this session.]*

## Approaching Holy Ground

Open with prayer, inviting God's presence and guidance during this group meeting.

## Building Community

- How hopeful do you consider yourself? Rate yourself on a scale of 1 to 10, with 10 being the most hopeful and 1 being the least. Why did you give yourself this rating?

- Think about the two questions posed in the Christmas letter near the end of chapter 9: (1) What is the good life? (2) How did you find out? Discuss your responses in pairs.

- Write any questions, comments, or issues related to the reading that you wish to discuss, and place them in the question box.

## Focusing on Scripture

[Before the session, write these Bible references on separate slips of paper: Psalm 130:1-8; Isaiah 40:28-31; Lamentations 3:19-26; Romans 5:1-11; Romans 8:18-25; 1 Timothy 6:17-19; Titus 2:11-14; and 1 John 3:1-3. Now, have participants work in pairs and have each pair select one or two slips of paper until all papers have been distributed.]

- In pairs, read and discuss the Bible verses you selected. What kind of hope does each passage portray? Summarize the object of the author's hope in a word or phrase. What meaning or inspiration can you draw from this passage? How does it relate to your own experience?

- Have someone read each Bible passage and report the pair's findings on the questions discussed above. [Using a marker, write the word or phrase summarizing the object of hope represented in each passage on a large sheet of paper. When done, display the paper where everyone can see it.]

- What do you hope for? Of all the hopes portrayed in these Bible passages, which one resonates most closely with your own yearnings? In what ways does your faith bring you hope?

- What other Bible passages are important to you as a source of hope? If time permits, look up and read to-gether several of these passages.

## Practicing Theological Reflection

- What did you learn about God as a child? What was your childhood image of God? How has your image of God changed over time?

- When you pray, to whom do you address your prayers? What other names do you use to address God or talk about God? What do these names imply about your image of your relationship with God?

- [If you have the children's book In God's Name by Sandy Eisenberg Sasso, read it aloud. Then discuss the following questions.] Which names for God in this book do you find most appealing? Why? What are some other common names for God?

- The Bible contains many different metaphors for God. List as many as you can. Which of these biblical metaphors for God is most meaningful to you? Why? Which of the metaphors provides the most hope?

- The stories of Frederick and Eleanor illustrate that hope does not deny the presence of hurt and brokenness in our lives. What makes some people respond with resilience to issues of suffering, fear, loss, and injustice? And what makes others despair?

- Tell about a time when God's hope helped you get through a painful situation. How does taking "the long view" of God's promises help you through difficult times?

- When have you lost hope? When has God seemed silent or distant to you at a time when you longed to feel God's presence? How did you regain hope and a sense of God's presence?

- As individuals, reflect silently on the following questions: "In what ways do you attempt to control or secure your own future? How might these attempts deny the reality of the hope God offers us?" Write your thoughts in your journal. If you wish, share your responses with the group.

- Do you ever use the language of "God's plan"? If not, why not? If so, what do you mean by the phrase? What do you think is God's plan for your life? How does it feel to believe that you are part of God's plan?

- [Open the question box and read any questions or thoughts that were submitted.] As a group, discuss any issues that have not already been addressed.

## Encouraging One Another

- Share prayer concerns with the group as you feel comfortable.

- As a group, pray with and for one another.

- [Collect the prayer cards, reshuffle them, and have everyone draw a new card.] Over the coming week, pray daily for the person named on your card. Write on the card any special prayer concerns of this person. Remember to bring the card with you to the next session.

## Looking Forward

- Over the coming week, reflect on what you have learned about yourself, your fellow group members, and your faith during this study. Write your reflections in your journal.

- [Explain that next week's closing celebration will include an "agape feast" (a Christian fellowship meal) in which everyone will partake of bread and water. The group may choose to also include fruit and cheese in the meal. Ask for volunteers to bring these food items to the next session.]

## Going Forth

Close with prayer, thanking God for everyone in your group and for the spiritual growth you have experienced together.

# SESSION 10

## CLOSING CELEBRATION: SHARING AROUND THE WELCOME TABLE

[Explain that this closing session will include an agape feast, or "love feast," a traditional shared meal of Christian fellowship modeled after meals Jesus shared with his disciples. Although bread is shared, the love feast is not the same as Holy Communion. Traditionally, agape feasts involve prayer, singing, testimonies, and God-centered conversation. Once the bread has been broken and passed, everyone may eat and drink freely during the remainder of the session. (Note: For more information on the agape feast service, see The United Methodist Book of Worship, p. 581.)]

### Approaching Holy Ground
Open with prayer, inviting God's presence at the welcome table you are about to share.

### Building Community
Recall the question from Session 1: In a typical week, how much time do you spend talking about spiritual matters?

- How have your answers changed since that question was first asked?

- Lately what events or conditions have prompted you to think about God? Talk about your experiences.

### Focusing on Scripture
Have someone read John 21:1-14 aloud. As you listen, close your eyes and imagine that you are one of the disciples in the story, tired and discouraged after a long night of unsuccessful fishing.

- As a disciple in the story, how did you feel when you realized that the stranger on the shore was Jesus? How did Jesus' appearance change you?

• In what ways do you feel the spirit of Jesus may have appeared to you during your time together in this group? What holy moments did you experience in the course of reading this book and reflecting on it together as a group?

## Sharing the Welcome Table

Sing (tune of the Doxology) or say the following grace aloud:

Be present at our table, Lord;
Be here and everywhere adored;
Thy creatures bless, and grant that we
May feast in paradise with thee.

*[Serve everyone a cup of water or lemonade. Break the loaf of bread and pass it around the room, each person taking a piece. As each person passes the bread, invite him/her to share insights on the following questions:]*

– What does "the welcome table" mean to you?

– How has this study group experience been a welcome table for you?

When everyone has received a piece of bread, eat the bread and drink the water or lemonade together. During the remainder of this session, freely and informally share the remainder of the meal (bread, fruit and cheese if you have it, water or lemonade, etc.) as you continue your discussion.

## Practicing Theological Reflection

• With which characters and stories in the book do you identify most closely? Why?

• Look back in your journal to your first session and read what you wrote about theology. Has your view of theology changed as a result of reading this book? If so, how and why? In what ways do you practice theological reflection in your daily life?

Have you been able to overcome any of the barriers to theological thinking that you identified in your first session? If so, how?

- Close your eyes and spend a few minutes reflecting on the eight spiritual yearnings described in the book. Then reflect on what you truly yearn for in your own life. Write your response in your journal. [*When everyone has finished, distribute the sealed envelopes from the first session.*] Open your envelopes. Talk about your spiritual yearnings with the rest of the group. How do your responses now compare to what you wrote back in Session 1? If your responses have changed, why have they changed?

- How do you think your participation in this group study will change you? How do you think you will apply what you learned as individuals? in your church? in your interactions with others at work or in the community?

## Encouraging One Another

- [*Collect and reshuffle the prayer cards. Have everyone draw a new card.*] In silence, think about the person named on your card and the gifts he or she has brought to your group. Then tell the group some characteristic of this person for which you are thankful.

- Share prayer concerns with the group as you feel comfortable.

- As a group, pray with and for one another.

- [*Distribute the prayer cards so that everyone receives the card with his or her own name.*]

- Take your prayer card with you. Keep it in your Bible or another special place as a reminder that you are part of a Christian community that loves you and prays for you.

## Going Forth

- Sing "Pass It On" or "Blest Be the Tie That Binds."

- Close with prayer, thanking God for this time of Christian fellowship and asking for God's ongoing presence and guidance as you continue to yearn for God.

## ABOUT THE STUDY GUIDE WRITER

**Tracey Henderson** is a Christian educator, curriculum writer, and candidate for ordained ministry in The United Methodist Church. She has done international development work in Mozambique and the Democratic Republic of the Congo and currently teaches International Studies at Waynesburg College and University of Pittsburgh. She and her family reside in Waynesburg, Pennsylvania.

# ABOUT THE AUTHORS

**Margaret Ann Crain** is associate professor of Christian education and director of deacon studies and Master of Arts programs at Garrett-Evangelical Theological Seminary, Evanston, Illinois. She is also coordinator of The Ecumenical Network for the Diaconate (TEND).

**Jack Seymour** is academic dean and professor of religious education at Garrett-Evangelical Theological Seminary. He has served as president of the Association of Professors and Researchers in Religious Education.

Margaret Ann and Jack are married. Both are ordained clergy and speakers for national events of Christian Educators Fellowship, the national convention of Deacons and Diaconal Ministers, and church and judicatory workshops. They coauthored two previous books, *A Deacon's Heart* and *Educating Christians*.

# Notes

## Chapter 1. Life-Shaped Faith: Theology in Everyday Life

1. Frederick Buechner, *The Longing for Home: Recollections and Reflections* (San Francisco: HarperSanFrancisco, 1996), 66–67.

2. Jack L. Seymour, Margaret Ann Crain, and Joseph Crockett, *Educating Christians: The Intersection of Meaning, Learning, and Vocation* (Nashville, Tenn.: Abingdon Press, 1993), 23.

3. John B. Cobb Jr., "Faith Seeking Understanding: The Renewal of Christian Thinking," *Christian Century* 111 (June 29–July 6, 1994): 642. See also John B. Cobb Jr., *Becoming a Thinking Christian* (Nashville, Tenn.: Abingdon Press, 1993).

4. From *The Book of Discipline of The United Methodist Church—2000* (Nashville, Tenn.: The United Methodist Publishing House, 2000), Part III, Section I, ¶ 125. Copyright © 2000 by The United Methodist Publishing House. Used by permission.

## Chapter 3. Yearning for Grace

1. Summarized by Pamela Paul in an interview on NBC *Weekend Today,* December 29, 2001. Paul conducted the study for *American Demographics* magazine.

## Chapter 5. Yearning for Justice

1. Philip Hersh, "In this day . . . why are we dying?" *Chicago Tribune,* 2 September 2001, 1, 16–17.

## Chapter 9. Yearning for Hope, Yearning for God

1. Substituting the term *kindom* for *kingdom* is an effort to use a more mutual and community-oriented image for the patriarchal image evoked by *kingdom* and *king.*

2. Roy and Dorothy Larson, Advent/Christmas letter 2001. Used by permission.

# DON'T MISS THESE UPPER ROOM TITLES

### Remembering Your Story
### Creating Your Own Spiritual Autobiography
### (Revised Edition)
by Richard L. Morgan

Best-selling author and workshop/ and retreat leader Richard L. Morgan offers readers of all ages a way to create their own spiritual autobiographies. Helpful for small groups as well as individuals, this resource leads you through ten weeks of study that include these topics:

Life stories • reclaiming childhood stories • family relationships
stories that connect generations • healing of memories

**ISBN 0-8358-0963-3 • Paperback • 176 pages**

### Leader's Guide
### Remembering Your Story

This revised Leader's Guide provides options for ten small-group sessions as well as for a weekend retreat. It includes group process, leadership ideas, and strategies for group formation.

**ISBN 0-8358-0964-1 • Paperback • 72 pages**

### *A Wakeful Faith*
**Spiritual Practice in the Real World**
by J. Marshall Jenkins

In this book, J. Marshall Jenkins assists us in recognizing ways the kingdom of God is flourishing in our midst and helps us to rouse and to deepen our hunger for God. With biblical grounding Jenkins examines the spiritual dimensions of alertness to God. He offers practical applications of spiritual wakefulness in daily living by showing how Jesus trained disciples to perceive the kingdom and to know God. Appropriate for individuals and small groups, *A Wakeful Faith* contains questions for reflections and discussion at the end of each chapter.

**ISBN 0-8358-0912-9 • Paperback • 218 pages**

To order these and other Upper Room products, order online at www.upperroom.org, call the Customer Service Department at 1-800-972-0433 Monday through Friday, or order through your local bookstore.